We Need to Talk

A straight-talking guide to raising resilient teens

Ian Williamson

Vermilion
LONDON

1 3 5 7 9 10 8 6 4 2

Vermilion, an imprint of Ebury Publishing,
20 Vauxhall Bridge Road,
London SW1V 2SA

Vermilion is part of the Penguin Random House group of companies whose
addresses can be found at global.penguinrandomhouse.com

Copyright © Ian Williamson 2017

Ian Williamson has asserted his right to be identified as the author of this Work in
accordance with the Copyright, Designs and Patents Act 1988

First published in the United Kingdom by Vermilion in 2017

www.penguin.co.uk

A CIP catalogue record for this book is available from the British Library

ISBN 9781785041051

Printed and bound in Great Britain by Clays Ltd, St Ives PLC

Penguin Random House is committed to a sustainable future for our business,
our readers and our planet. This book is made from Forest Stewardship Council®
certified paper.

The ... guid... substitut... other pro... Please ... treatmen ... up to dat... reader s... author ... arising ... tained in ... children ... are comp ... ...neral ... not a ... ceutical or ... locations. ... medical ... orrect and ... ge, and the ... ssue. The ... liability ... tion con- ... ntity of the ... this book ... iences. All

Contents

Acknowledgements

Much as I might like to think this book was created solely by me, the truth is that, without the help and advice of several important others, it would never have seen the light of day.

Candida Crewe, Damien Hirst and Helen Fielding offered help and sage advice on many aspects of the book for which I am eternally grateful.

I would like to thank my agent, Charlie Brotherstone, for making it happen and Morwenna Loughman at Vermilion for enthusiastically supporting the project.

Last but not least, I would like to thank my wife Emilia, who had to put up with me wittering on about the book for months on end and never once telling me to shut up about it.

Foreword by Helen Fielding – 2/10/16

Ian Williamson is a genius at understanding not only the problems (or, as enlightened parents call them, 'exciting challenges') of raising adolescents (or, as enlightened parents call them, 'sporadic lunatics') but crucially giving you practical ideas about how to do the job.

He has ideas which are much better for parents than flouncing out of the room shrieking 'I'm sending you to boarding school' then eating an entire family size bar of chocolate. And he tells you what they are, in user-friendly lists so in a moment of crisis, one can just run to the book, instead of the chocolate, and look it up.

Childrearing is not as it was. Children are not left free to roam around, potter about, and turn up again for supper. Technology has altered everything, the availability of porn has altered everything. Drugs have altered everything. Parental aspirations have altered everything. Gone are the days when children should be seen and not heard. Aspirational parenting culture involves a plethora of activities, texts, emails, electronic devices, and complex schedules which makes the job of a parent look more like that of an air-traffic controller.

Ian understands all this, and his guidance and suggestions work. He has spent twenty-five years at – as he puts it – 'the coalface' of modern childrearing. He writes with a refreshing straight-shooting style, full of humanity, reassurance and humour. Many of his phrases would sit well on a kitchen mug or computer mouse-pad:

'It is not an infringement of an adolescent's human rights to have to do what he is told.'

'They will respect you in the long run if you behave in a respectful way towards them.'

'Raising an adolescent sometimes seems to consist of a series of World War threes about nothing in particular.'

'Don't put their happiness at the heart of your parenting. They will feel a whole lot better about themselves and the world if you put preparation for adulthood as the priority.'

'Adolescents have their own internal logic, which isn't logical at all, being as it is, largely determined by what they want to have or do right now.'

'The three most important qualities, are a good work ethic, emotional resilience and a capacity to make and sustain relationships. If they have those in their locker going into adulthood they will do fine.'

'You don't have to persecute yourself if you don't get everything right. Good enough will do.'

This is a massively helpful, reassuring, and humorous insight into adolescence, as well as a stellar self-help manual. As a self-help book aficionado – as well as a parent – I would put it in my top ten all time greats and couldn't recommend it more highly.

Introduction

When I think of adolescence I think of a wonderful 13-year-old girl who came to see me after asking her mother and father if she could talk to a therapist about her 'worries'. Her parents were concerned. She seemed the most normal and happy of children; she was doing well at school and had good friends. Had they missed something?

No, they had not missed anything. Their daughter was having her first collision with adolescence. Hers was the most comprehensive and coherent account of the impact of adolescence on a teenager that I have heard before or since.

The girl sat in front of me with a look of bewilderment on her face ...

'What's happening to me?' she asked. 'It's like yesterday I was one person and today I am someone completely different. Something has happened to me. There used to be certainties in my life. I used to love my parents, go to church. I believed in God and was happy playing with my friends. But now everything's changed and nothing is certain any more. I feel angry with my parents all the time but I don't know why. I've suddenly begun to wonder

whether I really believe in God. And it gets worse ...
Everyone at school is talking about boys and sex. I don't
want a boyfriend, but should I have one? When do you
know you are in love? When do you decide to have sex?
I've also begun to worry about dying. Truly, my life is one
big mess. I want to go back to the old certainties. Honestly,
it's like a living hell.'

Nothing, quite *nothing*, can prepare a person for the trials
and tribulations of parenting an adolescent. A mother or
father can talk to experts and friends, watch documen-
taries and read manuals until they are blue in the face
and they might like to think they have it taped. But then
their beloved child turns 13 – or 11 or 15, or whatever
age it is – and suddenly life becomes a roller coaster, with
new stresses bursting out of the dark hither and thither,
grabbing and assaulting the uninitiated from every angle.
Whatever form their offspring's adolescence takes – and
the variety is infinite, I can assure you – no parent is spared
(even if they say they are), and there is never scope for complacency. Every parent can be absolutely sure that it makes
the strutting and tantrums and chaos of the toddler years
seem like a walk in the park.

As children grow older, the ups and downs of the
preschool years become a distant memory and usually
give way to a period of calm and order. Children largely,
although not always, do what they are told: they go to
bed on time, are generally cheerful and seem to accept the
family order of things. When they reach about 12 – and

sometimes younger – you might catch a glimpse, or more usually a whiff, of something changing. You know adolescence beckons. You've heard the nightmare stories from friends but you believe you've done a better job and it's not going to happen to you. It is a sort of conscious denial. But then the signs begin to become more frequent and intense. Over supper you discuss what might be wrong with your daughter. She seems distracted, moody and argumentative. Has something happened at school? Is she ill? The answer is none of the above. No illness. Nothing tangible has happened. She is simply becoming an adolescent.

What makes parenting during this period so utterly bewildering, exhausting and hard is the nature of adolescence itself. The sweet child, cooperative and biddable one day, is a cantankerous, argumentative pain in the neck the next. From the parents' point of view, there seems to be no rhyme or reason for these tectonic shifts in mood. There are, of course. They are called hormones, but they are invisible and work in unpredictable and mysterious ways. The adolescent's instability and swings and tempers can begin to completely dominate family life. The carefully constructed order and civility of the household, which had remained more or less intact for years, seems suddenly threatened by the actions of a mini, or in some cases not so mini, terrorist within.

It is worth holding in mind that, although it is mightily difficult for the parent, this period is also extremely difficult for the fledgling adolescent. This may not manifest itself in angry outbursts – although it often does – but instead in fear or anxiety and depression that arise out of trying, perhaps consciously for the first time, to make sense of the changes in their bodies and their place in the world.

But beneath the routine adolescent maelstrom that is complicated and challenging, there now lies a more insidious and worrying trend and it is one that we ignore at our peril. The number of adolescents suffering from mental health issues is increasing at an alarming rate. Consider some of the statistics:

- The YoungMinds Annual Report 2014 states that 1 in 12 adolescents self-harm.
- The number of adolescents admitted to hospital as a result of self-harm has increased by over 68 per cent in the last decade.
- The Health Behaviour in School-aged Children Survey 2009/2010 found that 30 per cent of adolescents reported 'low grade mental health' (i.e. they felt low, sad or down at least once a week).
- The number of adolescents with depression has nearly doubled in the last 20 years. Fifty per cent of those with lifetime mental health issues started having problems by fourteen years of age.
- Between 2005 and 2012 there was a 54 per cent increase in the number of children in the UK prescribed antidepressants.

The picture these statistics paints is a serious cause for concern. What is going on? By and large the teenagers of today are healthier and better educated than any previous generation. So what are these adolescents so depressed and anxious about? Are we missing something and, if we are, what is it and what should we be doing about it?

It is my view that we need to radically recalibrate how we are bringing up this age group. We need to focus less on the (inevitably elusive) provision of perpetual happiness and more on how realistically and securely to prepare our teens for adulthood. This should remain our priority in these testing years and is something I will come back to again and again in this book. As part of this we need to bear in mind the three most important qualities our teens need going into adulthood:

1. A good work ethic.
2. Emotional resilience.
3. A capacity to make and sustain meaningful relationships, not only with others, but also, of course, with themselves.

These are the crucial elements on which we as parents must concentrate if we are to successfully help navigate the well-balanced and stable development of our children. If you think that a less than demanding task then you have seriously underestimated the power of the technological revolution. Our teenagers nowadays are being lost to the addictive world of distractions and gratifications provided by electronic toys, online games, pornography, social networking, smartphones, and so forth.

Why Do We Need This Book Now?

As a practising child and adolescent analyst, most of my adult working life has been spent sitting in a consulting room listening to children and parents talking about their lives: the highs and lows; the triumphs and failures; the worries and traumas. Despite the insular nature of this working environment, I am at a sort of coalface and thus privy to the subtle – and not so subtle – shifts in the way the environment and prevailing culture impact on our lives.

Over the last years those shifts have been more seismic than subtle. What I seem to be witnessing is nothing less than a destructive attack on the way intelligent adolescents relate to themselves, to each other and to the world around them. This is happening not just to a minority of the many people that I see, but to each and every one of them. It is, quite frankly, ubiquitous, like a plague sweeping through my consulting room. I am in absolutely no doubt whatsoever that it will have serious consequences in the longer term.

The capacity of adolescents to sustain meaningful relationships with partners and friends both now and in their adult lives is being swiftly and systematically dismantled.

I believe it is not the historic hormonal havoc that is at the heart of adolescent struggles, although this plays its part, as it always has done. No, this destructive attack upon our teens' mental health is a result of contemporary forces far greater than a breaking voice, the development of breasts or the eternal desire of youth to push aside the influence of the older generation and forge their own way in the world. Our teens are at the very core of a communication and technological revolution that seems ever more incredible – faster, slicker, more realistic – and shows little sign of slowing down.

Most teenagers use their phones for 18 different activities; from photos to videos to social networking ... They are able to access these distractions, excitements and entertainments almost literally in the blink of an eye. Such is the all-encompassing nature of these irresistible new technologies that it is possible for our teens to delay, distort and even avoid any true engagement with the outside world and the people in it. Technology is a godsend to the adolescent, as those of you with teenage sons who spend their lives in their bedrooms playing computer games will know. Feeling frustrated or bored? Experiencing a difficult situation, worried or anxious? There is an instant route out of reality; just press the button and watch the screen with its alternative, more obliging universe explode into life. Lose yourself in it and – relief! – you can immediately reach the point of believing that the real world no longer exists.

What would happen to someone's relationship with the world and others if the whole of their life was devoted to meaningless distractions that once used to be the stepping stones between periods of deeper thought and reflection? What impact would it have on a person's capacity to think, to reflect, to *feel*? Indeed, what would happen to experience itself, if these meaningless meanderings became an end in themselves, and then a full-blown addiction?

In this new world it hardly constitutes a great leap of the imagination to realise that these adolescents are spending more time with their phones and computers than they are with people face-to-face, and that they are becoming more attuned to these 'toys' than to real human interaction.

Will it mean that their primary relationships will soon – if not already – be with their 'toys' as opposed to with each other? Is our relationship with our children being compromised by their relation to these machines? The answer is yes. An even more worrying question is whether our children's relationship to themselves is being compromised. And the answer to that, again, is another unequivocal yes.

Fast-forward to the next generation and what impact will all this have on our offspring's capacity to manage and process their own children's feelings and thoughts, if they have never learnt how to manage and process their own? And what kind of impact will this have on the psychological and emotional health of these children? How will they sustain a relationship with anyone if they don't have one with their own parents, let alone with themselves?

We need to get thinking about this, urgently.

However, there is no need to panic. If you get some idea of what is going on, what it is you are trying to achieve as a parent and how you are going to go about it, you will find the process of raising adolescents more enjoyable and less hazardous than you think.

How This Book Will Help

There are thousands of parenting books detailing how to deal with your developing child's every breath. In a way we mistakenly believe these books provide a sort of insurance against the mayhem that accompanies adolescence and indeed life. This is an illusion. I guarantee that when your much-loved teenager is out later than his curfew or is not picking up his phone, and the crazy fantasies about his imminent death start to swirl around your head, the fact that he was breastfed or fed on demand, or that you devoted your life to his every need, will be of no consolation whatsoever.

My ideas and thoughts about parenting have evolved over a long career working with children and their families, as well as from bringing up four children over the past 25 years. I would estimate that I have held 40–50,000 face-to-face consultations in my working life to date. This might not qualify me as an expert but the least you could say is that I've picked up a few things along the way.

This book is by no means comprehensive – you cannot magically become an effective parent just by reading a book, if anything because every child is different and the relationship between parent and child changes from week to week, day to day, and even from minute to minute (especially with capricious teenagers).

What we need to hold at the forefront of our mind is that our main job as parents is to prepare our children for adulthood and not to perpetuate some fairy-tale notion of perennial bliss. This cannot be done without a good deal of conflict. This book will guide you through many of the pitfalls of parenting an adolescent. It will help you sort out what to focus on and what to ignore. It will give you strategies to help you minimise those exhausting Groundhog Day encounters that are a feature of adolescence. Above all, it will help you understand why you are taking a particular line and as a result help you remain steadfast in the face of your adolescent's truculence and hostility.

Parenting adolescents has never been more challenging than it is today. It requires us to take positions on matters we have little experience, and even less understanding, of. It is my view that if you can focus on helping your child cultivate a good work ethic, develop emotional resilience and nurture their ability to sustain meaningful relationships then you won't go far wrong.

CHAPTER 1

What Is Adolescence?

Whenever we embark on a meaningful project, either personal or professional, the very least we do is give some thought to questions such as:

- What do we want to achieve?
- How might we get there?
- What resources might we need to get the job done?

The curious thing about parenting – probably the most important and demanding of projects any of us will undertake – is how little real thought goes into it. We invariably set out with a few books, a lot of advice and misinformation and, with any luck, a huge reservoir of love. If truth be told, from there on in we busk our way through it and hope for the best.

Once our children hit adolescence, however, the whole project takes on an unfamiliar shape. Tried-and-tested parenting strategies learnt in the earlier years go out of the window. The most ordinary of parental requests suddenly is to the adolescent an infringement of their human rights and would seem to give rise to World War Three.

What characterises parenting adolescents is its turbulence and uncertainty: the uncertainty of who they are and what they think and feel; the uncertainty of the future and who they will become. The turbulence arises as a consequence of the enormous upheaval that comes with adolescence and the compulsory nature of the process. The urgent need to try and make sense of it all gives the parenting work with them a compelling and intense quality.

Adolescence is rather like a compulsory train journey from somewhere comfortable and familiar to somewhere as yet unknown. There are hold ups, uncertainties, detours and breakdowns along the way, but eventually the teen will arrive at their destination: 'adulthood'. The really crucial point here is the compulsory nature of the process. The adolescent can't get off the train and they can't stop it. This is why there is such a lot of moaning and arguing, a lot of fire-fighting and gnashing of teeth, but not much in the way of a plan. It's exhausting not so much because adolescents are so demanding and chaotic, but more because we as parents are constantly in denial about what constitutes the adolescent process. We're always fighting it rather than working with it.

Adolescence is essentially a chaotic metamorphosis of mind and body. Much to our frustration as parents, it does not take place in an orderly or linear fashion. If you understand that internal and external chaos is the normal adolescent state then you will get a lot less stressed about your teen. So many of the mistakes we make as parents are futile attempts to eradicate the essence of adolescence. Time and maturation takes care of much of the irritating stuff, but if we spend all our time focusing on the wrong things we miss the really important things, like building a strong work ethic, developing emotional resilience and sustaining meaningful relationships. A good example of this is our attitude to mess; messy bedrooms and teens that don't clear up their mess. Mess is irritating, I grant you, but in the grand scheme of things does it really matter if your teen's bedroom is a tip? Instead, if your adolescent is cruising at school and just doing okay, I would argue that we then have an important issue to deal with.

The Adolescent Brain

For the parents of many adolescents the answer to the question 'What is going on in their brain?' might be 'Not a lot', but that would be a serious underestimation and, while the neuroscience might be a little dry for some, it's worth a brief look.

Dr Jay Giedd, a neuroscientist at the National Institute of Mental Health, Maryland, USA, used MRI scanning to unlock the workings of this complex organ. He discovered that a child's brain is not the finished article by any means. He noticed that there is a second spurt of intense activity that occurs during adolescence (the first winds down when children are very young, about two years old). During this period of intense activity, which peaks in the prefrontal cortex at around the age of 11 or 12, just as puberty is getting underway, the brain goes into overdrive. In a process known as 'blossoming', it produces branches at the end of the brain cells. These are called dendrites. What happens is that 'experience' causes the neurons to fire and the branch connections bridging one cell to another become stronger. Conversely, branches that don't fire, shrink, wither and eventually disappear. This process is called pruning. So it is that experiences (good and bad) crucially shape the neural networks and have a massive impact on how the adolescent brain is wired.

What this boils down to is that adolescence provides a window of opportunity within which young people fashion their personalities and outlook. We as parents have a very important role in managing this. Our interventions, our dialogues, our sometimes fraught and frantic attempts to get them to link actions with consequences, are absolutely critical to the way their brain gets wired. The way that adolescents manage relationships, communicate with others and see themselves, as well as their attitudes to impulsivity, and indeed to life, are a result of the triangular interaction between them, their environment and us.

This is where our management of technology becomes so important, a topic I will discuss at some length in Chapters 8 and 9. If much of this critical period is spent in front of a screen then it will undoubtedly affect your teen's neural network. Every hour spent in front of a screen is an hour of face-to-face time lost.

One circuit, for example, that develops in the adolescent brain is that which controls strong emotional impulses. The more we encourage adolescents to think before they act, the less likely they are to do something stupid. That's why it's important for us to keep banging our heads against those verbal brick walls that adolescents are so good at putting up. Accountability is the adolescent nemesis; teenage nirvana is a world without accountability. However, teenagers who are never held accountable for their impulses and actions have difficulty developing the control mechanism, which can have, at best, unfortunate and, at worst, tragic consequences. This is a painful and frustrating battle that often erupts into full-scale war as the adolescent rages against a world where actions have consequences. As a parent, you therefore have to be steadfast in your quest to push, pull or drag your adolescent into this grown-up world. Don't relent in the face of the 'I won't do it again, I promise' or 'Give me another chance' pleadings. Your sanctions or punishments don't have to be draconian but make sure you stick to them and don't back down. None of the consequences you give them will be as painful as the fallout from a real-life collision in early adulthood.

Parenting the Adolescent

A father came to see me about his 14-year-old son, Charlie. He was at a loss to know how on earth to deal with his behaviour. He seemed to be an involved and switched-on dad but his son's burgeoning adolescence had blown their relationship off course. Posturing and threatening behaviour on the part of his son had replaced the civility and order of their earlier relationship.

'It started a while back when I took him to his football club in the car,' Charlie's father said. 'He began to criticise my driving. He would give a running commentary throughout the whole journey: "You're over the speed limit", "You're driving too slowly", "We turn left over there." At the end, I felt like throttling him. He's 14, for God's sake, and he's never driven a car in his life! I told him as much but he had the cheek to tell me he'd learnt to drive on the Internet and was a much better driver than me. He was making a completely ridiculous argument but he clearly believed it. It gets worse. This has now spilled over into family life. He makes snide comments about everything I say and tries to undermine my authority with his two younger siblings. I am ashamed to say I lost it and walloped him. I'd just had enough.'

Charlie's story gives us a glimpse into the world of the adolescent. The familiar themes of grandiosity and belligerence come to life in his wrestling match with his father. Charlie's posturing and threatening behaviour is in reality a clumsy first attempt at exploring his developing potency and masculinity. A quality of these exchanges is that they are nearly always annoying or aggravating and they need to be handled sensitively. It is all too easy to 'cut them down to size', which is shorthand for humiliation. How else can your adolescent learn about how to be a man or woman? They need to butt heads with someone safe in order to explore and process their identity.

As one scrawny, challenging 14-year-old once said to me in a therapy session: 'You know you think you know everything, but I could take you out [beat me up] any time I want.' (To which I replied, 'We would both get into a mess if we tested that out wouldn't we, but I get your drift.')

I explained as much to Charlie's father and reassured him that his son's behaviour wasn't a sign of impending delinquency. I advised him to try not to get into a wrestling match or resort to punitive comments. I suggested he pay close attention but ignore it and, if he couldn't, then to make a gentle comment such as, 'You really want to wind me up today.' Whatever you do, I said, don't get into a wrestling match as it just makes matters worse.

If only it were that simple! The proverbial arm-wrestle is one of those rites of passage so common for parents of teens. I could write a book about all the ones I have got into with my own children, all of them pointless, infuriating and exhausting, and not one of them with a good outcome. So what are they about and what can you do to minimise their impact?

The first point to bear in mind is that it takes two to tango. In other words, your teen needs your full attention and involvement to generate the requisite emotional drama – it is critical for them to have an audience. So when you sense a confrontation developing, either walk away or, if you can't, stay neutral. If you do disengage your teen is likely to accuse you of not caring or not listening, plus or minus a bit of abuse. Don't rise to their goading; it's just a ruse to keep you in the game. Secondly, your child's rants are essentially monologues, a sort of adolescent stream of consciousness. If you keep butting in with your alternative view then the emotional temperature will inevitably go up. Remember, your teen wants an arm-wrestle not a constructive dialogue.

You won't avoid these conflicts completely, but you will lessen their incidence and their impact if you try to keep out of them. Try to remember that however defeated you feel you have one major advantage over your adolescent: adolescence is all about the 'moment' and your teen cannot see the big picture, while you most certainly can. So when you are in one of these confrontations and you appear to be losing, remind yourself that it's only a pyrrhic victory. Your teen will not have factored in that you can suspend their allowance, ground them or take away their mobile phone. Try to focus on the long term, not the short term.

Parenting adolescents is more difficult and complex than it used to be.

What has made the parenting of adolescents significantly more difficult and demanding over the last 10 years is that the two phases of adolescence (see Chapters 2 and 3) have artificially morphed into one. The onset of adolescence (usually around the age of 12, but sometimes earlier) is now accompanied by a headlong stampede into the world of adolescence proper (ages 15–19) with barely a pause for breath. There is no longer that vital incubatory period where the fledgling adolescent gains a chance to adjust to their startling hormonal changes, their new and emerging body and thoughts, and the demands that are being made of them from every angle.

The reasons for this are complex. The earlier and earlier sexualisation of the adolescent is one factor. But other developments, including the Internet – especially online pornography, smartphones and social networking sites – have catapulted the younger adolescent into the equivalent of Dante's inferno. Exciting though it appears on the surface, it is a world he or she is spectacularly ill-equipped to deal with. The often alarming speed of the changes to their bodies creates a generalised temperamental instability. It comes in tandem with separation anxieties and fear of loss, often experienced as insecurities about their identity and a fear of dying. There is also the thorny but critical issue of their sexuality to be sorted out. All told, this is a mighty project.

The spectre of sex and sexuality doesn't help matters, for it begins to infiltrate their thoughts and actions just when everything else is so unclear, and causes all manner of confusions. It is no wonder that at this age girls, especially, can become more prone than ever to eating disorders and acute worries about their bodies. Boys often develop compulsive and hypochondriac anxieties. Concerns about their virility and the strength and size of their penis also predominate during this period. These worries express themselves in the form of challenging, confrontational and ritualistic behaviours. It is as if boys need to test their strength and potency by bashing themselves against something stronger (more often than not a parent). It is irritating and upsetting but necessary.

So what is the fallout from all this change and how do we manage it? All of the above is the noise and background hum of adolescent development but what requires our attention as parents is the fallout from this psychological work. Boys often manage their anxieties through the adoption of grandiose thinking and omnipotent fantasies. Girls, on the other hand, become overly preoccupied with their bodies and how they look. They are often unable to exert much control over this way of thinking and being. As parents, we experience our teenage sons and daughters intermittently as inaccessible, unreasonable, moody and unreliable. It is possible to have quieter, less turbulent, even fun times during this phase, but you won't have much luck trying to bring continuous order to the proceedings.

Below are some tips on supporting your adolescent through this turbulent time:

- Try to enjoy the periods of calm.
- Try not to get too caught up in the hue and cry that accompanies this period otherwise you will find yourself

wound up in a lot of pointless confrontations. There is a downside to parents becoming too involved: you will give your adolescent too much power and this makes them feel more anxious.

- If you can, try and diminish the importance of the arguments by listening, acknowledging and empathising but, above all, keep calm. I guarantee this will be met with an emotionally heartfelt, 'You don't understand', but you never will in their eyes so don't try. Until your adolescent fully understands themselves, you won't either. Because of all this bodily and mental upheaval it is very hard to get resolutions to issues. That's why we often feel we are banging our heads against a brick wall. Don't take it to heart.
- Let the issues go once they are over and move on. Don't keep harping on about them as this just makes teenagers feel angry and humiliated.
- Instead, pay attention, keep a careful, non-intrusive eye on them and, above all, be available for listening. This takes a lot of time. Most of it will be fairly boring if truth be told but they do need you to listen as intently as you can manage.

In the midst of all this turbulence it's worthwhile holding these tips and questions in the forefront of your thinking. If you can keep your eye on the bigger picture it will help you work your way through the myriad of collisions, disputes, arguments and joys that characterise adolescence.

The Happiness Myth

The transition from child to adult is painful and difficult. Our job is not to smooth the path for our teen and give them a false sense of the world, but to help them navigate their way through it. Whether or not they are happy during this phase of their lives is, I'm afraid, beside the point.

Zara is 16 years old and, according to her parents, is decidedly unhappy and they are worried.

Her mother is tearful. 'I just don't understand what's the matter with her. We have given her everything she has ever wanted. We just want her to be happy,' she says. 'What can we do to make her happy?'

It's a fascinating question. What exactly does one do as a parent to make a 16-year-old happy?

When I see Zara she seems like a pretty normal adolescent. She is definitely miserable but she is not depressed. She doesn't think she is as pretty as her friends, she doesn't feel as clever as them either. She would like a boyfriend but the boy she likes doesn't seem to like her. She worries that she won't get as good grades in her exams as she would wish. Like so many of today's teenagers she has collided with the world of the ordinary, and it is painful.

The question is not so much what we can do but how we see and understand Zara's 'unhappiness'. The normal vicissitudes of adolescent life feel overwhelming for Zara. The job is not to somehow restore the Garden of Eden but to help her cope with life's frustrations and disappointments.

Our meetings are hard work because we are essentially working in different directions. Zara wants me to rescue her from what she feels are traumatic situations but which in reality are the normal stresses of life and I want her to develop some resilience.

In many ways Zara is a child of the times: bright, capable, but ill-equipped to deal with the challenges that lie ahead. She spends a great deal of time trying to persuade me she is depressed and needs to be on medication. Somehow, she believes, the medication will transport her seamlessly into young adulthood without actually having to do any of the psychological work or bear the frustrations that go with it.

'Ian, you don't understand, my life is a mess, I can't cope.'

'Zara, can you be more specific about what you are finding so difficult?'

'Everything. I'm depressed – I need to be on medication.'

'I think you are unhappy, Zara, but I don't think you are depressed and you don't need to be on medication.'

'You're not helping. What's the point of coming if you don't help?'

'Well, if you'd be more specific about what is troubling you I might be able to help.'

'I just hate my life.'

On and on we go. It's like an episode of *Friends* but without the humour. It was a struggle to keep her coming and an even greater struggle to get her to do any meaningful thinking. But about four months into the therapy we had a bit of an epiphany moment. She liked a boy but seemed incapable of thinking through how to get his attention.

'Zara, why don't you stop whining and do something about it? Go up to him and start up a conversation.'

'About what?'

'Schoolwork, the weekend ... anything will do, and if there's a gap in the conversation ask another question. Just keep talking.'

The following week she bounced into the consulting room with a huge smile on her face.

'It worked; I'm meeting him next week.'

From then on in the work became easier. Zara seemed to have realised that she needed to take some risks and roll with the punches.

What really helped, though, were her parents. Once they were reassured that Zara wasn't going to have a nervous breakdown they were much more able to stand firm in the face of her hysterical outbursts; this made a significant difference. Over the following year Zara calmed down, became more focused, more cheerful and much less 'unhappy'. She seemed more able to keep afloat without sinking into misery whenever she ran into difficulties. She stopped coming a week after her seventeenth birthday. I received a text message from her: 'Thanks very much, I'm fine now bye.' It was a messy ending, but it nearly always is with teenagers.

I did get a letter from Zara's parents a year or so later thanking me. She had done well in her A levels apparently and was looking forward to going to university.

Zara's story is illustrative of an adolescent problem that has become far too common. A style of parenting has evolved that dictates that the provision of perpetual happiness is an adolescent's inalienable right. This has of late been elevated over and above the long-held view that the primary role of parents is simply to adequately prepare their offspring for adulthood and to help them construct and maintain secure relationships. The vicissitudes of an adolescent's psychological life have been reduced to one single question: Is he or she happy? If the answer is no, we as parents feel we have resoundingly failed and are impelled instantaneously and shrilly to intervene.

The demand for happiness, as Pascal Bruckner, the French philosopher, writes in his book, *Perpetual Euphoria*, has become the new moral order and this is especially true of parenting, where the statement 'I want my child to be happy' is too often pursued with missionary zeal. If we mistakenly believe that the pursuit of 'happiness' for our adolescents is a realistic project, then it's legitimate to search for a manual that provides it.

Happiness as a right and a given is a curious misapprehension because, as adults, we know that happiness is nothing of the sort. Wisdom and experience dictate that it is, more, a fleeting sense of well-being, usually the bonus result of being engaged in something else. More often than not it is understood only in retrospect, as in, 'I was happy at such and such a period in my life', as opposed to having been fully acknowledged at the time.

So how has it come to pass that we parents, despite a logic that dictates otherwise, are of the opinion that our children should never 'suffer' a moment's misery thereby rendering them helpless when it occurs? There are two strands to this.

The first is that parents conflate happiness (which is understood as a continuous sense of well-being) with gratification (which is a need or demand instantly met, but is rarely more than momentary). These are very different notions. Adolescent behaviours, broadly speaking, can be divided into two polar opposites: teenagers are either in full flight mode as a means of avoiding frustration and responsibility or they are hell-bent on the pursuit of gratification as a way of not thinking. Getting in the way of either is what causes all the upset and conflict because these are what make them 'unhappy'. And yet we know that in their development towards adulthood it is critically important that they learn that they cannot have what they want all the time and that in order to become functioning young adults they must be able to manage the 'unhappiness' inherent in frustration and disappointment.

Second, it is not our attempts to make our teenagers happy that are the real source of the problem. It is our inability – even unwillingness – to help our adolescents appropriately tolerate and manage frustrations, distresses, disappointments and irritations that adds to the problem.

These very different emotional states are lumped together under the umbrella called 'unhappiness', a state that apparently demands immediate compensatory interventions on our part. Failure to intervene promptly and deflect this, we fear, might risk permanent psychological damage. The adolescent's loss of a mobile phone, for example, is enough to catapult the family into full-on crisis mode. Their life will disintegrate should they not be given a replacement within hours. Put simply, the tendency nowadays is to see an adolescent's upset and frustration as 'traumatic' in the long term as well as the short term, as opposed to something that is part and parcel of the vicissitudes of everyone's emotional life and merely what it is to be human.

The consequences of this muddled thinking cannot be overemphasised. Our fruitless and misguided pursuit of what we understand as happiness for our teen has blinded us to the more complex and diverse understanding of what they are really communicating and what they really need. What we should be focusing on is whether our teens are acquiring the skills they need to be functioning adults. While they are moping about the house delivering diatribes on their misery, their unhappiness and their boredom, we need to stay focused on whether they are fully engaged with their endeavours at school, whether their friendships are developing and whether they are avoiding or engaging with challenges.

Furthermore, the expectation that needs and demands must be met without delay (instant gratification) coalesces into an adolescent sense of entitlement. We have confused delayed gratification with real psychological suffering. When your delightful teenage son is driving you mad with his incessant demand for the latest 'must-have' pair of trainers, his angst in the face of your refusal isn't a sign of impending psychological breakdown. It is a collision with the more grown-up world of not always being able to have what you want when you want it. Far from it being a cruel deprivation, it is in fact a critical lesson in real life. Hold your ground. By allowing instant gratification, we run the risk of nurturing in the younger generation a view of the world that is not only unsustainable but also actively destructive with regards to long-lasting and intimate relationships. The space between what we want and actually obtaining it is where thinking, processing and connections between others and ourselves take place.

Learn to read between the lines

We need to be able to differentiate between our adolescent's frustration and anger, between his/her suffering and distress, between his/her sadness and depression. In other words, we need to help our teens distinguish between what is effectively a tantrum and what is of real concern. This enables them to relate to the complexity of their own psychological and emotional states. If we are able to get most of that right then it means that we can parent effectively. Most of your teen's angst is about avoidance. A rant about the pointlessness of school and qualifications is probably because they have a difficult piece of work due. You need to train yourself to read between the lines.

Before they get to understand themselves properly teens need us to do a lot of the 'making sense' for them. All teenagers are insecure, whatever their outward demeanour, for the simple reason that they haven't lived long enough and gained the requisite experience. This is why their lack of knowing so often feels to them like 'the end of the world'. In order to see the wood for the trees you need to do a little digging. If your daughter tells you she feels terribly alone, you need to get to the bottom of whether there is any semblance of truth to this statement. Have her teachers at school noticed anything? Have any other members of the family noticed anything? If she takes part in after-school activities, have those involved noticed anything? If the answer to these enquiries is that she seems fine, you can put her feelings down to teenage angst. If not, you may have to involve school or, in more serious situations, call in a professional. By all means take your teen's angst seriously, but do some checking first rather than immediately going for the knee-jerk reaction.

Not allowing your teen to do what they want will not cause lasting psychological damage.

Don't take your teen's rudeness, rejection and contempt to heart. The psychological and emotional work the adolescent has to do is incredibly demanding. They are trying to separate themselves from you in order to develop their own identity and world view. This is usually a rather unpleasant process involving a whole host of 'anti' behaviours. Your job is to facilitate this process while maintaining appropriate boundaries and respect. This takes years not weeks, so you need to be patient.

On top of the adolescent struggles and doubts, there are also the very understandable ones of our feelings in the face of fierce change and loss. Their burgeoning independence and nascent sexuality serves not insignificantly to add fuel to the fire of mayhem. We find it painful to have to contend with the shifting relationship with a child that was once taken for granted and so close. This bereavement is exacerbated if the parental relationship has become terribly strained. One mother said to me, tears in her eyes, 'We used to be so close. Now she rarely talks to me and, when she does, it's to tell me what an awful mother I am. It breaks my heart.'

Difficult though this is, the adult must do his or her best to help the child manage his/her feelings. It is not your child's job to take responsibility for yours.

The Emerging Adult

In an ideal world what kind of young man or woman would we like to see at the end of this process? First and foremost, I hazard, we would like them to survive it in one piece. If that seems like an overly conservative and rather too modest hope, I can guarantee that there will be at least one moment in the life of your adolescent when you will happily trade all your other more lofty hopes just for their safe return home. By nature adolescents are risk-takers and they do have an alarming habit of making the wrong call sometimes.

I imagine you would like your young adult to have a good work ethic. By this I mean they give of their best at whatever they take on. It's worth holding in mind that perseverance trumps talent most of the time. It's also likely that you would like them to have a decent group of friends who they are committed to and care about, and for them to have developed a degree of emotional and psychological resilience because, while we cannot guarantee their success in life, we can be absolutely sure that at some point in their early adult life they will have to deal with rejection and disappointment.

The development of psychological resilience should be one of the key goals of parenting adolescents and it starts with you helping them deal with all the less important rejections and setbacks appropriately. Adolescents nearly always find it hard to accept that things don't always work out as expected. Failure to deal with disappointment sometimes leads to a festering sense of injustice and grievance or, in severe cases, a 'the world is against me' frame of mind. Sympathy and understanding from you are fine, but your teen needs to get back on the horse so to speak.

Most rejections or disappointments of the non-traumatic kind emerge as a result of teenage group dynamics. The desperate need to belong often means teens are prone to endure unacceptable behaviours from other members of their friendship group. Remember that most teenagers don't know how to deal with these group upsets. As a parent, you need to help them process the problem. It will help enormously if you know who's who in the group, and if you think there is something dysfunctional going on in the group don't hang back from intervening. This is not an invasion of their privacy, it's being protective. (For more on friendships and dealing with group dynamics, see Chapters 2 and 6.)

Other disappointments, such as being dropped from the sports team, failing an exam or not getting a part in the school play, require a more robust response from you. By all means empathise with the upset, but don't let your teen slide into self-pity and don't let them quit in a fit of pique. Try not to spend forever ruminating on the unfairness of it all and instead focus on what they are going to do in response to the disappointment. To my mind these are critical lessons in learning the truth of the dictum that life isn't fair and will give your teen the confidence to deal with the more important disappointments later on in life. It's worth devoting a lot of time and energy to teasing out how they feel and how they should respond in certain situations.

If you are concerned about an issue in your teenager's life the first thing you have to sort out is whether it is a blip or whether it is more substantial. You can decide this by assessing incidence and severity. For example, if your teenager is unhappy 24/7, as opposed to once a month, then it's a problem. If your teen says they don't think that life is worth living but are partying hard by the weekend then it is nothing more than a glitch. At the normal end it may be that they are wrestling with an internal issue and it will be resolved quite quickly, while at the serious end, it may be the beginning of a depression. Start by trying to get your teen to talk about what is bothering them. However, be aware that their reluctance to accurately articulate what is bothering them is often simply because they really don't know, so you need patience and time. It is likely to be one of the following: friendship issues, sexuality, anxiety about self-worth or body issues. If your interventions don't relieve the worry enough suggest they talk to a professional outside the family.

Top Tips

- **You have to be clear about the scale of the problem you are dealing with.**
  Teenagers like their privacy, but if you feel they are withdrawing to their bedroom then you need to intervene. Don't always expect your concern to be welcomed, and don't allow yourself to be seduced by the notion that everything will be okay in the end.
- **Many adolescents do get depressed.**
  If you are really worried go and see your local GP. However, bear in mind that taking medication has its downsides, namely deciding when your teen should come off it.

Noticeable symptoms of depression in teenagers can include:

- continuous low mood or sadness
- voicing/showing feelings of hopelessness and helplessness
- frequent tearfulness
- being irritable and intolerant of others
- apparent lack of energy or motivation, and little or no enjoyment of things that were once interesting to them
- slowed movement or speech
- changes in appetite or weight (usually decreased, but sometimes increased)
- frequent unexplained aches and pains
- disturbed sleep patterns (for example, problems going to sleep and/or waking throughout the night, particularly in the early hours of the morning)
- losing interest or being disruptive at school or playing truant
- constantly complaining that they feel bored or lonely

[Reproduced from http://www.nhs.uk/Livewell/family-health/Pages/worried-about-your-teenager.aspx]

- **If your teenager is 'depressed' when they have to do something they dislike and fine when they don't then the chances are they aren't medically depressed.** Being miserable is not the same as being depressed.

- **Not giving your teenager what they want all the time doesn't cause problems, but indulging their every need does.** If you provide instant gratification then you are perpetuating an infantile world that leads to a severe case of 'entitlement'.

- **The angry outburst that results from not getting what they want is not a sign of impending psychological disorders, it is a tantrum.**

- **You need to keep an eye on how your teenager is responding to setbacks and disappointments.**

Being a teenager is too stressful for there to be too many prolonged periods of happiness. Bouts of unhappiness come with the territory; they are not automatically a sign of an impending mental health issue.

CHAPTER 2

The Younger Adolescent

The challenges posed by the younger adolescent (ages 13–14, but sometimes as young as 11) differ hugely from those of the older adolescent (ages 15–19). One word sums up the whole psychological terrain of this age group: insecurity. The first hormonal surge propels the fledgling adult into a completely unfamiliar world. They are often at a loss as to how to deal with what is happening to their bodies and their minds. This causes all sorts of problems; the main ones being anxiety and insecurity. Once upon a time there used to be a sort of incubatory period, which allowed the adolescent time to get used to these changes, but there has been a huge culture shift in the last decade which means young teens now stampede into full-on adolescence.

The sometimes rapid change in their bodies at this age creates an unsettling sense of 'not knowing who they now are' which is why they can spend so much time worrying about their appearance. The urgency of the need for answers and resolutions to questions about body and mind is what makes parenting them so difficult. They want solutions to things that will only be resolved with time. They know this but their inability to deal with it creates discord and arguments. These bodily changes usually lead to periods of intense self-consciousness often accompanied by vulnerability and shame. A look or an innocently-made comment can trigger a huge blow up; you need to tread very carefully with regards to body matters.

Friendships

Tim is struggling, as are his parents. He is a young 14-year-old and things at school are not going at all well. He is neglecting his work and messing around. His school is a tough one and there are huge social challenges to negotiate. But, when I see him, I quickly pick up on the fact that the work issues pale into insignificance compared to those associated with his group of friends. As far as I can understand, his chosen cohort has trouble written all over it, being as it apparently is full of minor delinquents. They do all the things other adolescent groups do, but then they take it that bit further: Tim tells me they have taken to breaking into empty office sites and vacant buildings at night. I note there is a cruel edge and slightly dangerous quality to their carryings-on. Nevertheless, Tim hangs on to the group. Unfortunately, it is pretty plain that he is one of the weaker ones as well as desperately wanting to be a player. Sadly from Tim's point of view the reality is that at this stage he just makes up the numbers.

Physically Tim hasn't taken off yet. His face is covered in teenage spots and he has that familiar young teenage look: none of his clothes quite fit and his hair is a total mess. Like so many of his age group he is self-conscious to the point of paranoia. I can see why all this bothers him. The rest of the boys in his group are physically much further advanced and are already young men. This lack of confidence leaves Tim feeling vulnerable. Lack of confidence at this age often exacerbates the adolescent's need for acceptance and confirmation of self from the group (this is something I will come back to later in the chapter, page 40). It is precisely this that makes them vulnerable to being used by other members of the group for nefarious activities.

Tim's parents are focused on his poor work ethic at school and haven't given much thought to his friendship group. They berate Tim endlessly with our favoured parental tactic – the monologue – and I understand why. They feel helpless in their efforts to positively reconfigure his psychological landscape. Their hearts are in the right place but, unwittingly, their efforts are just pushing Tim further into the arms of the group. Over the weeks, in my consulting room, I get to know the members of the group, albeit Tim's version of them. Tim is besotted with them. In his eyes they are cool, fearless and exciting. I see it somewhat differently: they are reckless, careless and untrustworthy. This is precisely the kind of misperception that is common with this age group. There is one slightly older boy who worries me. He is manipulative, controlling and cruel – all in the name of having a good laugh, needless to say. Tim is blind and, at 14, why would he be able to read the runes?

The denouement, when it came, was, predictably enough, painful and final. The gang drank some alcohol, got a bit drunk and the manipulative character asked to borrow Tim's mobile phone. He wrote an obscene text and sent it to one of the female teachers at the school, whose number he had managed to obtain, and then deleted the message. Of course, the text was sent from Tim's mobile and a quick call identified him immediately. The following day he was summoned to see the Head Teacher and expelled on the spot. Tim protested, but there was nothing to exonerate him. He refused to implicate his manipulative 'friend' for fear that he would be expelled from the group as well as from school.

Tim and his parents were both very shaken by the experience. It was an adolescent prank that went badly wrong. Adolescent boys love pranks. The excitement and the thrill they bring are intoxicating. If the group is relatively normal their pranks are usually harmless but if the group verges on the delinquent they easily get out of hand, as Tim's experience shows.

Thankfully Tim's black cloud had an extraordinary silver lining. A new school meant Tim had the opportunity to make new friends. Arriving with the tag of having been expelled from his previous school immediately afforded him 'cool' status in the eyes of some of his new peers. In the intervening period his growth spurt had kicked in and at last he looked like a proper young man. He was now a revered figure at the new school without having had to do anything and he quickly dumped his former group of mates. When I saw his parents during the half term they reported that he was a different boy, more confident and assured. They had had their fingers burnt once and weren't about to fall into the same trap and so were much more involved with his new group of friends. However, it doesn't always pan out as well as it did for Tim.

The friendship group

In the early stage of adolescence friends become increasingly important and the adolescent group starts to play a bigger part in the teenager's life, as Tim's story makes clear. This is the serious beginning of their relational life outside the home and how it develops depends to a large extent on their physical development and what kind of relational life the teen has had at home with their parents and siblings. The physical disparities between teenagers at this age can be huge and bring added pressure to their already fragile relationships. Early physical development is often a source of envy for the later developer and it can confer imaginary power both on a physical and a sexual level. Tim's decisions were tied up with his physical immaturity and his desperate wish to be 'someone'.

To understand why life is tricky for younger adolescents, it is important to bear in mind the anxieties that the fledgling adolescent is experiencing: their fear of being alone or of being left out, intense insecurity and huge levels of self-consciousness. These states of mind drive them to seek sanctuary in a group, often around someone whom they believe embodies the essence of coolness, which loosely translates as someone who at least gives a good impression of having these anxieties taped. It is an illusion, of course, but the younger adolescent doesn't see that. To be accepted and feel part of the group is all that matters and this often puts him or her under huge strain. The more insecure and the less confident they feel about themselves, the more pressure they are under to adopt the values of the group, which at the early stage demands absolute conformity. In these situations the teenager effectively hands over sovereignty of self to the group in exchange for acceptance. You can see this most clearly in the formation of gangs, but the same dynamics operate for teenage groups albeit in a much less extreme form.

How your young teenager manages this early foray into group life will tell you a lot about how well placed they are to manage the next stage of adolescence. Everything they have learnt or acquired at home will now be put into practice outside the home, for better or for worse. However well you think you have done it is unlikely that these early encounters with the real world will be trouble-free.

Confidence, for example, is a critical issue. Too little or too much of it can cause problems. Some children by nature lack confidence and, for some, fear of failing and rejection play a part in this. Solid confidence comes as a by-product of overcoming hurdles and meeting challenges. Learning to read, swim, ride a bike or play an instrument are all important building blocks. Similarly, playing in a sports team, singing in a choir or acting in a play are all activities that are worth their weight in gold, psychologically speaking, when your child takes his or her place in the group. These groups, with their clearly laid out structures and 'rules', and an adult in charge, prevent the manoeuverings and machinations of the more disruptive members. They provide a haven where adolescent confidence can flourish.

On the flip side, overconfidence can also be a problem and often results in recklessness, impulsivity and poor decision-making. If you feel that your teen is exhibiting any of these characteristics consider grounding them. By all means talk to them but in my experience talking doesn't change behaviour, grounding does.

Although teenage groups are often supportive, after a fashion, they are nearly always messy, transient and unstable, sometimes thoroughly unpleasant and occasionally cruel. The reason for this is that inclusivity is extremely fickle in groups at this age and the prevailing dynamic is more to exclude someone who, at a whim, they feel doesn't fully represent the group's culture or 'look'. The realisation by its members, if a barely conscious one, that they are leaving what is with any luck a secure home environment, creates even more anxiety. These children are effectively in a psychological no man's land, neither secure in themselves or their attachment to the group nor completely comfortable in the family environment. The fear of what lies ahead varies from individual to individual, but for some it can feel overwhelmingly frightening and can result in a retreat from life in the hope that they can stall the developmental process. Boys disappearing into their bedrooms to play hours of computer games is a good example of this retreat from real life.

What should we be doing as parents while this is going on? It is important to hold in mind that young adolescents are trying to get a handle on what is, from their point of view, total internal confusion. As I said before, activities such as sports, music and drama play a crucial part here. They provide a much-needed buffer against the vagaries of the adolescent group. Don't let your teen give these activities up if you possibly can.

Such is the power of the group culture that it can take precedence over family life. Don't let it: don't be intimidated by the argument that if you don't let them go out all the time with their friends they will be social pariahs forever. There is time enough for adolescent life, but spending time as a family is still crucial at this age. There is room for both.

Although it won't always be immediately obvious that your teenager is having trouble with one or several members of the group, it is well worth establishing who the movers and shakers are; who the good guys are, who the wild ones are and who the undesirables are. Encourage them to come round to your house so you can take a good look at what's what and who's who. If you feel someone has trouble written all over them, don't hold back from intervening, even if it means stopping your adolescent from socialising with them. This will undoubtedly cause friction but that's a small price to pay for your child's safety. I have lost count of the number of times parents have said to me,

'I just can't believe my son could do such a thing. It was so cruel to gang up on that little boy and beat him up' or 'I am shocked at the pictures. I wouldn't have thought my daughter was capable of such stupid and inappropriate behaviour.'

The best friend

Certainly, not all adolescents join specific groups and there are some who opt for the best friend strategy. This looks from the outside to be a much less risky proposition but it is, in fact, largely a defensive stance and can be fraught with problems. Adolescents often get together on the basis of common interests but in reality they are bound, if unconsciously, by the fear of being alone. It is risky because it is a case of having all their eggs in one basket. What happens if the best friends fall out with each other, or one of them finds an alternative best friend, or leaves to join a group? If your teenager only has one or two friends you need to try to encourage him/her to widen their sphere in whatever way they can, maybe by trying for a sports team or joining a drama class or choir.

Without question, your teenage child needs to be part of some sort of group or have close(ish) friends, as no one can be expected to pass through this phase of their life alone and without some sense of belonging. The group of friends is the entity that enables them psychologically to move away from home and to forge their own identity. For a period of time this group will assume centre stage in the adolescent's life. The challenge for teenagers is that they have very little experience to draw on to manage group life, even more so if they are an only child, so they need a lot of practical help sorting out what to do and what not to do. This has to be learnt from us. Those interminable conversations about who said what and to whom need careful listening to and, as parents, we need to offer advice. Your teen needs help talking through the inevitable social exclusions and fallouts. This can be hugely time-consuming but it is crucial to your teen's secure psychological development.

The Role of Social Media

Social media can play havoc at this age as many of your teen's anxieties are relayed minute by minute to anyone who wants to read about them. A misplaced comment, a slight or being excluded intentionally or unintentionally can really take its toll on the confidence of the more fragile teen. It is so important, therefore, to help your teen manage themselves online. It's my view that you have to have an electronic shutdown in the evenings, not as a deprivation, but because your teen needs respite from the all-pervading modern technology. Imposing an electronic ban will not necessarily be warmly welcomed by your teen, but it's critical. It's also important to never allow your child to have passwords on their electronic devices. Again, they will more than likely kick up a fuss invoking the familiar adolescent protest of invasion of privacy. Don't buy it. Explain that you will check their online browsing history from time to time, and wiping it clear is an indication that they are on sites or engaging in searches that may be inappropriate. Some of you reading this will probably feel a little uncomfortable with this level of intrusion. In my view it's a matter of love and care. Of course your teen isn't going to like it but, as I have made clear, whether they like it or not shouldn't be part of your decision-making. For more tips on online safety, see Chapter 8.

Top Tips

- **Try and slow down their manic dash for freedom.**
  This is not an easy task. Not allowing your adolescent to do what they want to do will provoke outrage and conflict. Firstly and importantly take them seriously. It's easy to poke fun at their clumsy attempts to appear grown-up. They easily feel humiliated. Listen carefully to their request but simply state that you don't feel they are old enough or experienced enough to be allowed to do it. Don't argue, don't go into long explanations and don't negotiate. This won't stop the stampede but it might help to slow it down.

- **How good is their judgement of situations?**
  Do they, by and large, make good decisions or are they impulsive? If they are prone to impulsivity then you are going to have to rein in their freedom for the simple

reason that they can't manage it. There is no doubt that this will be hard work but it needs to be done.

- **How dependent are they on their friendship group and what is their role within it?**
  You need to keep a very careful eye on these groups for the reasons outlined above.

- **Get some idea of their level of confidence by monitoring how they operate inside and outside of school.**
  If they aren't confident you have to give them some help. Get them to join in an activity (it doesn't matter what) and make sure they are trying hard at their studies. You may encounter some resistance but if you persevere you should be okay.

A huge amount of learning about relationships takes place during this phase of your child's life. This learning is best done face-to-face with family or friends.

CHAPTER 3

The Older Adolescent

While the pain of psychological and physical adjustments dominates the early adolescent years, the older adolescent (ages 15–19) presents very different parenting challenges. This is the time they need to perform. By this I mean that most of the developmental preparation should now have been done – at least theoretically – and the fledgling adult must now perform without the aid of his parents. Whether this is academically, socially or sexually, the pressure is on. All the tricks and bluffs will count for nothing in the face of real-life challenges. If we have done our job well enough as parents (note that well enough is good enough), if we have kept in mind the primary aim of parenting which is the preparation for adulthood and if we have ditched our misplaced obsession with our teen's perpetual happiness, they will come through this.

In many ways the relative quiet and order of this period is deceptive. The previously volatile younger adolescent will have matured to a certain degree, they have become used to their bodies and, while their management of themselves and their lives leaves a lot to be desired from our point of view, there are definite periods of calm. The erratic storms of early adolescence are largely a thing of the past. Admittedly, the bust ups, when they come, can be brutal and painful for both parent and adolescent, but they tend to lessen in the face of the need to deal with the real-life challenges that confront them. The deception is that in the managing of themselves they have learnt to be better at covering up the bits that aren't so well adapted. As a consequence, we can be quite easily duped if we are not paying attention: the anxieties associated with sex, excessive socialising, drinking, promiscuity and taking drugs can camouflage insecurities about self-worth and potency; last-minute preparations for exams disguise anxieties about true self-worth; and retreating to the bedroom and immersion in computer games may indicate frantic attempts to stall the developmental process.

Alice is 17 and in the last year of her A levels. She goes to a good all girls' school where expectations are high. She has always been an outstanding student and never really caused her parents or the school a moment's worry. One might be tempted to think of her as the perfect child. Alice is an only child of older parents and they are devoted to her. She is their 'project'. So far Alice has met all her parents' expectations. She has given them everything they have wanted but I wonder at what cost.

Adolescence is not about giving parents what they want; it is about preparation for adulthood. I note with interest that Alice seems not to have indulged in a moment's rebellion during her adolescence. Bizarrely, from her parents' point of view, she seems to be going off the rails just at the time when she needs to be at her best. She has become friends with some wilder girls from another school and is going out a lot. Neither her mother nor her father is really sure what she's up to. She has changed her look and her attitude. She had been quite a conservative girl, bookish and not obsessed by fashion. But she has given herself a radical makeover: she has cut her hair short and dyed it a sort of red. Her form teacher was somewhat shocked by this development and had rung her parents to explore what was going on. Although she is still performing at school, her academic position is more precarious than it should be.

When I meet Alice I am confused as her radical look is at odds with her manner. She is tall and slim, and her short dyed hair gives her an edgy look, but this is in complete contrast to her timid, bland vacuous manner. Although she is obviously bright, she doesn't really offer anything that suggests she is her own person or even has her own ideas. She seems to be a follower rather than an 'initiator'. I receive flaky responses to my questions about what might be going on. There is a lot of shoulder shrugging and smiling but nothing of substance. I suspect she is giving me what she thinks I want. However, I see a glint in her eyes when I ask about her new friends. I can see why she finds the wilder girls so enticing and exciting. She is desperate for some excitement and exploration in her life. In many ways, Alice is more like a 13- or 14-year-old. She has bypassed or avoided the turbulence that accompanies the early adolescent years, but she is certainly gearing herself up for some 'fun'.

Alice's parents don't have any experience of dealing with adolescent conflict and they have an enormous amount of their own well-being invested in Alice's education. She is expected to go to a top university and they are anxious that it may all go wrong. I suspect it is this which Alice has unconsciously tuned into and may explain why she has been so reluctant to rebel and follow her own path. The damage the adolescent project may cause her parents is too much for Alice, as it is for many adolescents whose parents' lives are too heavily invested in their children's success.

I lay out some ground rules for them to think about:

1. Alice is only allowed to go out once a week.
2. If her grades don't improve she will be grounded until they do.
3. If she doesn't start paying more attention at school then her summer plan to go off for a week with her friends to Ibiza is not going to happen.

Mild though these suggestions are, I can see her parents are taken aback by the lack of 'wriggle room'. We discuss the need to get Alice's full attention as we don't have time to waste.

I offer to tell Alice the ground rules myself which both parents seem pleased about. I call Alice in and spell out the deal. She naturally bristles with indignation. I see a side of her I haven't seen before. Gone is the bland, diffident Alice. Instead we have a properly truculent adolescent in front of us. Her look and manner are now in synch. Alice is all outrage and bluster. She then plays what she thinks is her trump card.

'Suppose I don't agree to these rules. You can't make me stay in. I'm 17. I can do what I like.'

I can see her parents are taken aback by her forthright position.

'That's true, Alice,' I counter, 'but only in one sense. All behaviours have consequences. If you choose not to abide by the rules there will be sanctions.'

Alice is incandescent. She protests that it is not fair and storms out of the room in tears of rage.

Her parents are shocked. They have never seen Alice so angry. They are shaken by her outburst. But after some discussion they do nonetheless agree to follow it through. We decide that I will meet them regularly in order to help them manage the situation. It becomes clear over the coming weeks that the parents struggle to remain firm in the face of Alice's tirades. They broker deals when perhaps they shouldn't (don't we all?) but to their credit they largely stick to the plan. Alice made a desultory attempt at rebellion but she was smart enough and mature enough to work out that the only person who was going to suffer was herself. One of the advantages of dealing with older adolescents is that they are more amenable to reason sometimes.

The strategy held up and Alice did well in her A levels. Not as well as her parents had hoped, but she ended up at a good university. To my mind that was a good outcome.

Older adolescents worry parents in a whole host of ways of which their younger counterparts can only dream. We know the enormity of the real challenges that face the 15–19s. We also know we have fewer tools and strategies to help them manage. Their age and relative sophistication means that 'pushing them around' or issuing edicts doesn't work. To a large extent they are on their own. It's not quite cross your fingers and hope, but it is close. Eventually even the most conservative and strictest of parents is going to have to let their teen free.

When you see your older, physically mature adolescent strutting their stuff it is worth bearing in mind that their confidence is paper-thin. They live in fear of not meeting the unspoken behavioural expectations of their peers. A mistake, a social gaffe, a joke not understood or a social rejection quickly leads to intense feelings of shame and ridicule. This will test their emotional resilience and the more fragile and sensitive may withdraw to their bedrooms. They need you to be attentive without being intrusive.

With this age group it is worth holding this thought in your mind: if everything seems to be going well the chances are you are missing something. The reason I write this rather odd statement is that it is a quality of this group that they are masters of deception. They know what it is you want to hear and they are usually sophisticated enough to know how to get round any rules you may put in place. It doesn't mean you have to automatically distrust them but you have to be canny and smart. Don't allow yourself to be seduced by complacency. Here is a checklist to help you identify whether your older teen is in need of intervention:

- Are they putting in effort at school?
- Do they have a good group of friends?
- Are they engaged with the world and its challenges?

If you have a yes to all three of these questions, and by that I mean hard evidence not their say-so, you and they are on the right course. If you answer no to one of these questions then you need to do some thinking about how to change the situation.

I see a lot of older adolescents precisely for the reasons outlined above. It is show time and they are in a panic. Their problems broadly fall into one of two categories:

1. They have stage fright (low confidence, low self-esteem).
2. They haven't learnt their lines (they have bluffed their way through or used avoidance tactics and are now in a panic that they are going to be found out).

The truth is that even the most confident of adolescents will struggle to some extent. They are too inexperienced in life to be certain they can make a success of the challenges they are about to face. Bravado, avoidance and lethargy are often the preferred coping mechanisms. Don't be fooled or distracted by these behaviours; panic is never very far away. At this stage the parental pep talk or angry outburst are rarely if ever useful, for the simple reason that the adolescent hasn't a clue how to tackle his or her problem. You need to be specific. In other words target the problem. It usually means getting them to face up to whatever is frightening them – and that fear is usually fear of failure – and developing a strategy that tackles it.

How to Communicate With Your Teen

Patience and timing are prerequisites for dealing with this age group. If you want to have a talk with your teen about their behaviour then you are not going to have much success if they are in the middle of a row with their boyfriend. You have to wait until you can get their full attention. That an incident or issue feels urgent to you isn't a useful factor in deciding when to intervene. A badly-timed intervention just creates more aggravation, so ensure you time it right.

How do you do that? It is impossible to go through every possible scenario here, but there is one critical question you need as parents to be clear about: do you have your adolescent's full attention and cooperation in trying to deal with this issue? If you do, fine. If you don't, what do you have to do to get it?

Getting your teen's full attention is more difficult than you think. If it's an issue they don't want to deal with then they will indulge in all manner of avoidance tactics. If they are preoccupied with something in their life then you will get short shrift. I would suggest that late evening in the middle of the school week might be the best time to attempt a conversation. Keep your intervention short and to the point, and don't lay on guilt or offer practical help. For example:

'Look, you're leaving your homework to the last minute and creating unnecessary stress. Why don't you try and get it done as soon as you get it? I can help you with the organisation if you like.'

'Why don't you turn your phone off while you're working? Getting distracted all the time means it will take twice as long.'

'You aren't trying hard enough at school. I know what that's about; it's about being scared of failing. I've done it myself, it doesn't work.'

All of the above open the way for a longer, extended discussion at another time.

In my experience parents often find it very difficult to intervene effectively at this age. Why parents struggle like this is complex. Partly it is because they have become used to dealing with a more 'civilised' presence in the family. They have survived the endless aggravation of the earlier teen years and are enjoying a more peaceful life. Sometimes it is as a result of their own experiences as a teenager, this is especially true if their parents were harsh and unforgiving. It may also be a result of feeling that the fallout may turn out to be irreparable and they will lose their child forever. Other times it can be an irrational fear that children will leave home or never love them again. Whatever is driving their response you can be sure it is has nothing to do with the adolescent they have in front of them.

Here are some tips for dealing with confrontation:

- **Try not to lose your temper.**
  However, if venting your spleen makes you feel better by all means go ahead but don't expect it to make any lasting difference. The more drama there is the less likely it is that there will be a positive outcome. The more defensive and guilty a teenager feels the less cooperative they will be.
- **Don't expect logic to prevail.**
  Adolescent logic is driven by impulse not reason. This is why monologues and lectures rarely have an effect.
- **However much conflict there is between you and your adolescent there have to be rules.**
  Disagreements/bad tempers/moodiness, even low-level rudeness are okay. Being disrespectful (for example, calling mum a 'bitch') is not. Make that absolutely clear.
- **Try and avoid making your teenager feel guilty.**
  All but the confident few are already overwhelmed with inadequacy and ramming it home just creates resentment.
- **If you are going to have any success with an intervention, you have to get your adolescent's full attention, so choose your moment, sit them down and above all be firm without being angry.**
  Remember that even the most confident and belligerent of adolescents are paralysed without the two 'Ms': mobile phone and money.

The problem with this age group is that we don't have much time. Interventions are difficult to effect. They require the adolescent to agree to engage with the problem and, if they don't, then you as parents have few options. For example, if you find that your adolescent is procrastinating with homework you need them to agree that they need your help before you can get in the door, so to speak. If they keep blocking you, you have to somehow find a way to get their attention. One good way of trying to effect change is by reining in their omnipotence. By this I mean the way they live their life is totally dependent on you as parents, a fact that they conveniently overlook. If you withdraw your support, financial or otherwise, the whole project grinds to a halt. This will get their attention and give you an opportunity to make changes. The importance of Alice's story is that it illustrates the need for parents to intervene quickly and firmly in the face of problems. Cosy chats and negotiations are not going to get the job done effectively enough.

Here is a reminder of what we, as parents, need to be focused on. … It is important at this age that your teen is trying hard at school, regardless of outcome. If they don't/ won't step up to the plate then consider limiting their freedoms. At this age their job description looks something like this: 'If I put in my best effort at school then I am entitled to some freedom at the weekend.'

Monitor how your teen is responding to challenges. Again, try making their freedom dependent on their involvement in something. It doesn't matter much what it is but it has to be challenging.

If your older teenager is withdrawing from relationships you need to seriously consider professional help. There may be complex underlying issues to do with sexuality, or equally difficult issues around fear of rejection, or even fears about sex itself. Your adolescent may find it easier to talk to someone outside the family about these things.

Top Tips

- **Don't mistake bravado for confidence.**
- **Make sure they are engaged with their life inside and outside the home.**
  It is important to respect their need for privacy, but don't let them opt out of family life completely by shutting themselves in their bedroom and avoiding every family gathering.
- **Keep an eye on their work ethic.**
- **Monitor how they are coping with rejections and failures.**
- **Never fall for the age-old adolescent mantra that they are the only ones being deprived of an experience which in their eyes will lead to permanent social exclusion.**
  See it instead as an important introduction into your adolescent's elastic relationship with truth.
- **What they think they can manage and what they really can manage are different things entirely.**
  The gap between the two is vast, and you have to be on hand to help reconcile the one with the other.

Remember adolescence is a long process. Don't worry if you get things wrong. Doing your best is good enough.

CHAPTER 4

Behaviour

Parents of teenagers frequently ask me what behaviours they should be worried about and what they should let go. This is a really good question. The adolescent maelstrom is so frequently overwhelming it's often hard to know where to start.

Max's story is a classic example of what I am referring to. In fact it might be titled 'A treatise on what not to get involved in':

Max's parents are sat opposite me. His mother is trying to remain calm but she looks as if she is about to explode. His father has his elbows on his knees and his head in his hands. He stares at the floor as his wife tells the story.

Max is 14, the eldest of three boys and, as far as I can gather, has been a relatively good boy until recently. By all accounts he is a bit of a live wire and cocky with it. He was suspended for a week from school for having some pornographic pictures on his mobile phone and there was a minor dispute with another boy, which the school thought merited another day or two at home. Neither of these offences strikes me as being a major cause for concern, more a result of the poor judgement his age group is renowned for.

However things took a turn for the worse when Max's mother found cigarettes in his school bag one day while looking for his homework diary. She was taken aback and confronted him. The sensible option was for Max to own up and take the punishment, but we are talking about teenagers here and the sensible option more often than not goes missing at crucial moments. So Max started digging a hole for himself and told her he had no idea how the cigarettes got there. Max's abnegation of any responsibility is a familiar one and is guaranteed to ratchet up the aggravation level. Having started digging he kept going. He told her they belonged to someone at school who asked him to look after them but he couldn't remember who it was. In time-honoured adolescent fashion his efforts to extricate himself from this mess by adopting an 'It's nothing to do with me' defence had precisely the opposite effect. His mother was now incandescent as he had added 'lying' to the charge sheet. Max is a bright boy and, as all adolescents do when faced with losing the argument, he upped the ante. In this case he went into a rant about his many and various grievances with his parents and ended up storming out of the house. His mother's fury dissipated quickly enough when he didn't come home for his supper and was replaced with worry when he didn't answer his mobile phone. One of Max's brothers unhelpfully stoked the fire with the suggestion that she call the police as someone might have kidnapped him.

Dad returned from work and walked innocently into this mess, blissfully unaware of the crisis that was about to engulf him. His wife launched into a truncated version of the story and told him that he needed to go and find Max immediately. Dad was caught off guard and hadn't had time to properly digest what had gone on but he sensed his wife's anxiety and went looking for Max. In truth he was less than enthusiastic about the task. After a hard day at work this was the last thing he wanted to be doing. He quickly realised that Max was more likely to be at a friend's house than tramping the streets and he eventually found him at his friend Eddie's house.

When he arrived the boys were happily playing computer games in the living room. Max warmly greeted his dad as if nothing had happened and, of course, in Max's mind nothing *had* happened. Like all teenagers, his time frame and memory of events had undergone a radical transformation in the intervening two hours. The cigarette saga and fall out with his mother was but a distant memory. Being able to finish the computer game was now his central preoccupation. But Max's dad was still fed up and hadn't really got up to speed with this vital change.

'I think we need to go, Max,' said Dad.

'Can't you wait half an hour while I finish this game?'

Max's dad was momentarily taken aback by his son's cheek. However, being in someone else's house inhibited him from giving Max a piece of his mind.

'No, we really have to go. Mum will be waiting and I have things to do.'

Max was unperturbed.

'She's not going to die if we get back half an hour later.'

Max seemed rather pleased with himself and nudged his friend as if to make sure he had got the joke.

Much to Dad's annoyance Eddie's mother helpfully offered to bring Max back when they had finished playing.

'No that's very kind of you but Max really must get home now.'

He leaned forward to squeeze Max's shoulder, signalling that he meant business.

Max shrugged him off.

'Okay, I'm coming, you don't have to hit me.'

Dad ignored this wind up.

Max picked up his jacket, half-heartedly said his good-byes and slouched out of the house.

As they walked to the car Max started up again, the simmering frustrations of not being able to finish his computer game coming to the boil.

'You always spoil things. I'm never allowed to have fun. It's so boring at our house.'

'Max, please leave it.'

'I have my rights.'

'Max, I said leave it. It's been a long day at work and I'm tired.'

'It's not my fault. Why don't you get another job?'

Max's dad snapped. He reached over and slapped his son across the shoulder.

The sudden force of his father's reaction shocked Max. As he got into the car he pulled his jacket up over his face and sobbed quietly all the way home. Once home he ran upstairs to his bedroom and slammed the door shut.

Max's mother came out to see what all the fuss was about. Her husband recounted the story but failed to mention the altercation. She was hugely relieved that Max was safe and rushed upstairs to see how he was doing.

Within minutes she was back downstairs in full war mode.

'Did you really hit him? Don't you know how damaging that is?'

Her husband, in an attempt to downplay the incident, suggested that Max was making a meal of it.

'Well, did you hit him or didn't you?'

'It was more of a slap than a proper hit,' Dad countered.

'It's the same thing. I just can't believe you did such a thing.' And so on.

'Anyway that's why we are here, Mr Williamson. We have been arguing for weeks about this incident. I cannot believe my husband hit him, I just can't get over it.'

'I admit I lost my temper,' said Max's father. 'I'm not proud of it but you're making too big a deal of it. Max is making a meal of it. Anyway it was your fault the whole thing escalated in the first place. Was there really any need to make such a fuss about the cigarettes in his rucksack?'

The dispute went on like this for quite some while before the situation calmed down and Max's parents could look at the incident more dispassionately. In essence both parents had been caught on the back foot by Max's antics and hadn't been clear in their own minds what to let go and what to attend to.

This kaleidoscope of familiar parenting mishaps perfectly illustrates the problems of exercising parental authority over a teenager. It takes the parents of teenagers several bruising encounters to realise that the previous 'Do as you're told' version of authority is more or less redundant and they are in much more complex territory. Max's story and all its ramifications was wholly avoidable, as are most of the countless 'Max-type' incidents we have all endured as parents of adolescents.

Before we look at the story in some detail I want to make a seminal point that needs to be hardwired into the brain when parenting teenagers:

If you feel yourself being swept along by your adolescent's drama, bail out and give yourself some time to think it through. You cannot exercise authority over your adolescent if he/she is running the show. Let it go, give yourself some space to process it and come back to it later.

This is the major mistake Max's parents made. They ended up as actors in a play that Max was directing. This is a recipe for disaster.

Let's look at some of the critical points in the story.

Max's mother gets the show started. She is shocked and upset that he has cigarettes in his school bag. Max on the other hand is cross with himself for being so stupid as to have left them there. In that moment the tension is escalating – his mother is on the attack and Max is on the defensive. This rarely has a good outcome with teenagers. Was it really such a big deal for Max to be caught with cigarettes in his bag? Teenagers smoke; sometimes it's a phase, sometimes it becomes a habit. But whatever your view you aren't going to successfully engage a defensive adolescent.

She might have said something along these lines.

'Look, Max, I don't know who these belong to. I hope they are not yours but if they are you need to be careful. It's a hard habit to kick and you know the health dangers.'

'They are not mine Mum, I told you.'

'Okay, Max, I hear you.'

Situation over. (Mental note to parent: need to talk to Max about the perils of smoking at another time.)

Next up Max's mum decides to escalate the dispute. If you are going to escalate a dispute make sure you are ready to deal with the consequences. Escalating a dispute is a risky business because most adolescents have a limited capacity to deal with feelings of guilt, shame or failure. These are often felt as grievous assaults on their fragile sense of self and they go into defensive mode very quickly. Max took a familiar course of action. He raised the ante again by storming off.

This manoeuvre by Max is a game changer. He creates a completely different narrative by storming off. In two hours his mother goes from fury with him for smoking/lying about smoking to worrying about his safety. He has changed the whole nature of the interaction.

I suspect Mum is anxious but also angry with herself. She recognises that she should have probably made less of a scene or at the very least de-escalated the situation, but it's too late. At that moment her husband walks in and she blindsides him.

Dad isn't really paying attention and is fed up with having to deal with the problem after work. He is still not up to speed when he finds Max at Eddie's house. He hasn't properly registered that Max has moved on and the issue is that he is now deeply involved in a computer game. Eddie's mum offers him a way of resolving the issue but he ignores it, feeling that Max's procrastination is an affront to his authority. The two of them are now angry with each other, Max is spoiling for another fight and Dad duly obliges and rises to Max's bait and the fall out leads to the current predicament.

With a bit of work, once Max's parents had calmed down, they were able to see how Max had played them like a violin. It happens to us all.

As with all matters adolescent, the waters become muddier the more we delve into them. Part of our effectiveness as parents is diminished by the fact that a lot of the time we cannot decide what is worth fighting about and what's worth letting go. Some of our decisions are informed more by what we ourselves did as teenagers as opposed to the nature of the adolescent we have in front of us. Any hint of a lack of clarity or hesitation is seized upon by the adolescent and invariably leads to all the familiar and tiring arguments.

Two factors are worth bearing in mind when you have to make a decision:

1. What sort of adolescent do you have?
2. Is the activity age-appropriate or not?

If you have a son or daughter who is impulsive and prone to making bad decisions, or is easily led and rather immature, then it makes sense to err on the conservative side in what you allow or don't allow them to do. This is in order to protect them, not to curtail their freedom. Adolescents of the more impulsive persuasion don't take kindly to having their freedom curtailed, but you need to be realistic and hard-nosed about this. The decision needs to be made on the basis of their behavioural track record, not on the strength of their arguments as to what others their age are doing. A persuasive but erroneous argument I have heard from parents is that they need to treat their children in exactly the same way. This makes perfect sense in theory, but in reality children are treated differently and so they should be because they *are* different. What works for one child won't work for another. The fact that it might not be perceived as fair is a very good life lesson for your teen and an irrelevance in deciding what you will allow for your adolescent.

To help you gauge when to raise an issue with your teenager and when to back off, I have listed below some things you should worry about and things you can probably let go.

What You Need to Worry About

Let's start with three serious concerns. I am not going to elaborate on them too much as we all recognise them as causes for concern. Suffice it to say that if you are worried about any of these you need to go to your GP in the first instance.

Self-harming

Self-harming is on the increase for both boys and girls. It is a very complex issue and a full discussion of this topic is beyond the scope of this book, but, briefly, there are three main reasons why adolescents self-harm:

1. Low self-esteem: as in, 'I am rubbish and I am going to hurt myself as a result.'
2. An inability to deal appropriately with anger; turning it against the self.
3. Dislike or hatred of one's body.

If you suspect your son or daughter might be prone to the above it is worth keeping a careful eye open for unusual marks or scratches. If you suspect them of self-harming don't beat about the bush. Confront them in a serious but non-persecutory way. You need to be sensitive when raising this with your teenager because they will feel intense shame about what they have done or are doing. Adolescents are very anxious about their mental health and most know that self-harming is a sign that something is very wrong with them. In the first instance take them to see a GP who will in all likelihood refer them to a professional.

Anorexia and bulimia

Many teenage girls, and boys for that matter, mess about with their food and worry about their weight. The bodily changes that accompany adolescence can cause any number of psychological anxieties and it is usually the trigger for eating disorders. In some instances it can be a response to peer pressure, while in others it is tied up with familial relationships. It can be a phase but it can also become serious. Again, take it up with your teen in a non-persecutory way, but whatever you do don't ignore it and hope it will resolve itself. If you begin to notice serious weight loss or you are worried then go to your GP who will refer you to a specialist.

Drinking and drugs

Taking drugs, like drinking, is a rite of passage for many teenagers. For some it's more enticing than for others. Where you position yourself depends on knowing your adolescent. By that I mean the one you have in front of you, not the one you wish they would be. Many parents get in a muddle about this. You have to be honest. If your teenager is prone to being impulsive, is a bit of a risk-taker or has low self-esteem then alcohol and drugs may become an issue.

In my experience the younger adolescent will want to experiment, which I see as part of being this age. In all likelihood they are going to try one or other, or both. It is a matter of education, so you need to talk to them about drink and drugs, but I wouldn't get too stressed out about it unless you suspect they are regular users. For the older adolescent it can become a lifestyle choice that masks insecurity and lack of confidence. If you are concerned then again go to your GP. It is worth holding in mind that independence for the teenager comes with responsibility. If they are coming in drunk from parties every weekend or you sense they are taking a lot of drugs, ground them as they are not holding up to their end of the deal. Intervening by grounding or removing mobile phones and money will cause a huge furore, but it is worth nipping it in the bud. Whatever you do don't stick your head in the sand on these issues.

Less Serious but Needs Attending To

Not sleeping

Adolescents need huge amounts of sleep so they need to be able to get to sleep in the first instance. If they can't it may be a symptom of something else. In my experience it is either a symptom of something that is worrying them at school, friendship troubles or they are too wound up from using screens. You need to do a bit of careful detective work on the former two and put a limit on the latter. Texting friends while in bed at night is a favourite activity for teenagers and one that can severely disrupt their ability to get to sleep. As I mention in Chapter 8, I am in favour of teenagers handing their phones in at night. There is no compelling reason for an older teenager to take a mobile phone to bed with them.

Too much reliance on gaming and computers

The rule of thumb is this: can they stop with a gentle nudge from you? If they can, fine; if they can't, you have a problem to deal with. (See Chapter 9 for more guidance.)

Poor effort grades

Don't fall for the simplistic view that poor effort grades are a sign of laziness; it is more complex than this. Poor effort is often much more to do with fear of failure or fear of the challenge. If left unchecked it can corrode self-esteem. Make sure you make clear to these adolescents that you are less concerned about achievement grades but 'demand' that they put in their best effort. (See Chapter 10 for more advice on this.)

Avoiding challenges

Make sure your adolescent is engaged in something challenging. To a large extent it doesn't matter what. This is important, as they need the confidence that comes with making a decent fist of a challenge. As they become young adults the challenges will come thick and fast. If they don't have resilience or a confidence in their ability to get over obstacles they will be vulnerable to life's setbacks.

Lack of friendships

Do they have some friends? This is important because adolescence is difficult to get through without them. If they don't have friends you need to explore why this is the case. Sometimes it is to do with not being able to manage the sharing that friendships entail or they may feel too shy and lacking in confidence to try. Encourage them to join an activity where they can meet others in a non-stressful way. This might help them learn the skills needed to make friends. (See Chapter 6 for more advice on helping your teen to build meaningful friendships.)

Withdrawing from life

If your adolescent starts to withdraw from life (stopping activities that they previously enjoyed, dropping friendships, etc.) and spend increasing amounts of time in their bedroom, you need to intervene. This is a fear-based behaviour. Something is troubling them. The reasons why this might be the case are endless: they may have fallen out with their friendship group; they may have been bullied; it could be that they are taking drugs; they could be worrying about their sexuality; they could be spending too much time playing computer games ... Whatever it is withdrawing doesn't solve the problem, it just puts it on hold and the longer the 'withdrawal' goes on the harder it is to solve the original problem. It may also be a sign that your adolescent is depressed. It is worth consulting a professional if you can't get to the bottom of it.

Can they do the deal?

Sooner or later you will have to do a deal over curfews. This is the first real test of whether your teen can link freedom with responsibility. If they can stick to the curfew given then fine, but if they can't they are telling you that they are too immature to link the two and you have to ground them until they can. No discussion, no argument. (See Chapter 5 for more guidance on this.)

Things You Can Let Go, More or Less

Sleeping late

I know it can be irritating when your teen wanders downstairs at about 2pm and starts asking for breakfast, but in the grand scheme of things it's probably not worth getting too stressed about. They will grow out of it eventually.

Mess

Mess and adolescents go hand in hand; their rooms can resemble a war zone at times, boys more so than girls. By all means try and get them to tidy up but don't get too stressed if it feels like you are banging your head against a brick wall with this one. This is another one they will grow out of in time.

Irritability and bad temper

Someone once described the state of adolescence as being chained to a madman for a few years. The combination of hormones and psychological and academic challenges are often overwhelming for even the most placid of teens. Don't take it personally and don't deliver lengthy monologues. They are only too aware of their inadequacies and failures; all you are doing is rubbing salt into the wound. By all means bring their attitude to their attention but keep your interventions low-key.

Selfish behaviour

Selfish adolescent behaviour is annoying and upsetting and often leads parents to question what they have done wrong to have raised teenagers so oblivious to the needs and feelings of others. Structurally adolescent selfishness is intrinsically very different from other types of selfish behaviour. There are so many internal changes going on both physically and psychologically that they have to be 'preoccupied with self' to be able to work it out. Once they get a handle on what's going on inside them they can get their head up, but it takes time. Excessively selfish behaviour is often a sign that they are struggling to deal with what is going on inside them, so rather than focusing on the behaviour see if you can get to the bottom of what's troubling them. This is the 'art' of parenting a teenager. Timing is everything here. It is fruitless to sit them down whenever you feel like it and start asking what's wrong. You have to sense when they are ready. For example, when your adolescent son unexpectedly comes out of his bedroom at 10.30pm and plonks himself next to you on the sofa, it probably means he wants to talk. A tentative opening remark like 'Is everything okay?' sets the scene. If he hesitates before brushing you off, you can guess that everything isn't okay. That's your opportunity: 'You don't sound too sure about that.' Hopefully a discussion will then follow. Many parents tell me that their adolescent doesn't open up, but it is usually because they keep missing the moment.

Lethargy and lack of enthusiasm

Teenage lethargy is draining to say the very least. They can suck the life out of the most joyous of experiences. A much-looked-forward-to holiday is often felt to be the most boring event on earth for an adolescent. This is a temporary phase and not worth getting too wound up about. The reason for the malaise is that, although it isn't always obvious, the 'internal work' (Who am I? What do I want?) is their major preoccupation and often leaves them oblivious and disinterested in family life. Gentle humour is a better way of dealing with this than going overboard about their attitude.

Rudeness/surliness

Rudeness is part of a group of 'anti' behaviours that are generally a pain in the neck. What often makes it even more galling and perplexing for us is that teens are invariably paragons of good behaviour and manners when they are with adults outside the family. The rude behaviour arises largely as a consequence of the separation process. In order to separate from much-loved parents it is necessary for your teen to distance themselves and what better way to do it than by being disrespectful and surly. This does not mean it should be tolerated but how you tackle it is important. By all means draw their attention to it, coax and cajole, but try to avoid lectures and stern monologues. This behaviour will pass once they have separated themselves sufficiently.

Lying

All teenagers lie, period. Their relationship with the truth is elastic at best. Their accounts of life outside the home are laced with inaccuracies and fantasies. So let's ditch the idea that some adolescents do and some don't. As parents we are all in this together.

There are usually three underlying motives for lying;

1. They don't want you to give an opinion on what they are up to.
2. They don't want you to know what they are up to.
3. They don't want you to know where they are.

If you have the fortune/misfortune to catch them out in their lie, ditch the moral outrage and concentrate on the central issue, which is that lying undermines trust and trust is crucial if they are to have independence. All but the most disturbed adolescents have a powerful conscience and they will respond to this quite quickly if you can get the tone of your language right.

Stealing

I have written about this in more detail in the next chapter (page 90) but, briefly, this is not a sign of impending delinquency. It is more often a reaction to the constraints of entering a world where they can't have everything they want. This is a painful process and needs to be handled sensitively. If you go in too heavily you will exacerbate their already intense feelings of shame. The real fallout from stealing is that it damages your teen's sense of self-worth. When you scratch the surface they often 'hate' themselves for having done it, so try to be matter of fact when confronting them. Make a plan whereby they can make good what they have done (reparation) and make clear that whatever they might gain from stealing is not worth the damage it does to their sense of self-worth.

Top Tips

- **Don't sweat the small stuff.**
  They will grow out of it eventually.
- **By all means indulge yourself in outrage and long monologues, but it does very little good.**
- **If you know or sense something serious is up with your adolescent contact a GP or a professional straightaway.**
  Don't fall prey to that old wives' tale that they will grow out of it eventually and do nothing.
- **Finding the right moment to talk to your adolescent is all about timing.**
  Try and develop that skill.
- **Don't go overboard about lying and stealing.**
  Do your research and focus on the central issue, which is trust.

It's impossible to completely avoid becoming embroiled in the mayhem of adolescent-life, but if you can take a minute to assess what is and what isn't really important then you will worry less, have fewer confrontations and enjoy these years together more.

CHAPTER 5

Crime and Punishment

Jonny is 15 years old and, to all intents and purposes, is a good kid. He does his homework and seems to be getting along reasonably well with friends. He has two younger, beautifully behaved (apparently) sisters. Jonny is about to introduce the family to the world of proper adolescence. Like most parents colliding with the teenage world for the first time, it has come at them out of the blue. They hadn't given it a moment's thought. One minute the family are in cruise mode, the next it's World War Three. Jonny has, according to them, morphed into a horrible brat almost overnight. He hasn't, of course, it's been brewing for months, but they, like so many of us, just ignored it. His parents have become exasperated by his intermittent rudeness and refusal to tell them what he is up to when he is out. I ask them to give me an example. They tell me a typical adolescent story.

Jonny is going out more and more, later and later, and they are worried. Just saying he is 'with friends' is not enough for them when they haven't a clue who these friends are and what they are doing when he is with them. I ask them if they have tackled him about it.

'We did and he just said, "Fuck off, it's my life, I can do what I want with my free time." We just couldn't believe what we were hearing.'

Jonny's textbook adolescent outburst has blown a hole through the civility of previous discourses. The old prototype for relations between child and parent has been ripped up.

I asked them what happened next. Jonny's mother explained how her husband gave him a good talking to and threatened to stop him going out if he didn't start behaving.

'What did Jonny say?' I asked.

'Well, nothing at first,' said his mother, 'and I thought for a moment that we were getting somewhere, but a few minutes later he flew into a rage and started ranting on about the fact that we never give him any freedom, how we are always interfering in his life and none of his friends tell their parents what's going on. Then my husband became more and more angry and they ended up having a shouting match before Jonny went upstairs and locked himself in his bedroom.'

There is nothing that exercises the parental mind quite like the topic of crime and punishment. We plough our way through the muddle of the early years and then begin the magical teenage mantras, 'Why should I?' or 'You can't make me.' It is then that our best laid plans and noble intentions go to pot. We see children's behaviour as the barometer of our effectiveness and worth as parents. A well-behaved child is testament to our skill and expertise; while bad behaviour advertises parental failure. It is the cause of endless arguments between parents: others – always others – are too lax, too strict, too emotional or too inconsistent. But we all get it wrong at times. Most of us think we are being rational, clear-sighted and logical, but we are not. Show me a parent who isn't occasionally swayed by the intensity of his or her feelings, or grossly upset by the behaviour that confronts him or her, and who doesn't react in a way they know isn't ideal but is prompted by the heat of the moment.

The truth is we dispense justice randomly although we think we are being even-handed and we cannot resist going in for retaliation. We don't care if it is not the 'right' thing to do, when pushed too far, we damn well will give them a taste of their own medicine, usually to let off steam and make us feel better. In short, most punishments are more for our benefit than for that of the offender.

In my consulting room over the years, accounts like Jonny's have been told to me countless times. Jonny's story encapsulates so many of the features of adoles-cent–parent relations. There's the broadside, obviously – the lecture delivered by the father – but it serves no purpose whatsoever other than making the adolescent more angry. I have delivered more of these than I care to remember and every one has been a waste of time. And there is Jonny's irrational rant masquerading as truth. He has twisted a normal parental concern about his safety and whereabouts into a furious outburst about them being overprotective and intrusive. He wants to be free to do what he wants without constraint – that plaintive, age-old adolescent cry for independence without responsibility – and then there is the inevitable stalemate. Nothing has been resolved. Groundhog Day is just around the corner.

The Point of Punishment

Before exploring the nature of managing adolescents and outlining a few guiding principles, I want to take a slight detour into the area of punishment because parents of adolescents often become fixated on it. Parents erroneously believe that the right punishment will teach their teenagers a lesson they will never forget and, bingo, they will have eradicated adolescent maelstrom and everything that goes with it in one go. It sounds ridiculous, I know, but I could write another book about the lengths some parents have gone to 'eradicate adolescence'. I've tried eradicating it myself on more than one occasion.

One of the better ones was the story of the exasperated father of a delightful but irritating 15-year-old. After one nasty bout of metaphorical butting heads with his son, the father sat him down and in a fit of pique told him that if he didn't pull himself together he would send him to live on a sheep farm in Western Australia. He thought he had finally found a vaccine that would cure the illness. The following week I received a call from his wife cancelling our next meeting. With some trepidation I asked her what had happened.

'My husband feels completely humiliated and can't face the next meeting. Our son just laughed when he heard the Australia threat and told his father he needed to get some psychological help.'

Amusing though this story is, how many of us, driven to distraction by our adolescent, have threatened something equally crazy?

The psychological point of punishment is that it relieves the child of guilt. By this I mean their bad feelings about themselves. This is the price they pay for having transgressed and their guilt can be expunged by a suitable sanction. That, in a nutshell, is the sole purpose of punishment, and don't let's be under any illusions otherwise.

What punishment does *not* do is teach your child a lesson or act as a deterrent. This is because adolescents are a work in progress and any lessons, such as they are, will only be learnt over a long period of time. The adolescent life is lived in short time frames that are often disconnected. This is why we feel so exasperated when they commit a 'crime' days after having been punished for the same offence. Such lessons are determined by maturational processes rather than any punishments you or I can come up with. What is more, there is a definite downside to punishment, and it is an important one: what arises from excessive punishment is fear, loathing and resentment. Always has, always will. And that is a very high price to

pay for obedience. What we do after the punishment is
what matters. And this is the rub – the talking, the discussing, the arguing that should come after the punishment is
tiring and time-consuming, and we would often rather be
doing something else.

That said, part of our role as parents is to provide an
environment in which our children can learn about functioning effectively in relationships and in groups. This
means that their needs and wants have to be shaped and
managed. This often involves conflict and difference and,
as a consequence, punishments, to an extent.

Here are some of the issues worth thinking about
before delivering punishments:

- The most important thing I have learnt about managing
  adolescents over the years is that it is a battle of inches
  gained and lost and, therefore, the most precious qualities you need are patience and stamina. You are in for the
  long haul. Any worthwhile adolescent will cause you
  quite a bit of grief but one of the Achilles heels of the
  adolescent is that they can't cope with the long game.
  Losing your temper or getting het up over every trans-
  gression is a waste of your time and energy. In short, pick
  your battles.
- If you yourself need affirmation from your adolescent,
  you are going to get into a hell of a mess. I understand
  that we all need to be loved by our children or at least be
  shown some appreciation, but it is not appropriate for
  them to bear the burden of dealing with our own insecu-

rities or anxieties. Adolescents are not generally known for outbursts of gratitude.

- Adolescents by nature are chaotic, messy and unreliable. Concentrate on the big issues and don't go overboard on the small things (see Chapter 4). This stance will make for a smoother ride.

- When parents say, 'She just doesn't seem to care what punishment we give her,' it is never as simple as it may sound. What it actually means is that she doesn't care about herself and that needs dealing with forthwith. Adolescents *should* care about what happens to them, and most of them do. The point is that they are not *showing* you that they do and, if they are going out of their way to do the opposite, something is up and you cannot afford to take their lack of tears or contrition at face value. Sometimes their petulant display of indifference reflects such a dislike and/or low opinion of themselves that you have to think about it hard and explore why they are saying they don't care. The answer is usually complex. Reasons for apparently not caring might include: an excess of aggression in the household which they begin to mimic and then direct towards themselves; the burden of unduly high expectations, expectations which they feel can never be met; and/or chronically low self-esteem as a result of neglect. For any of these, you may wish to seek the guidance of a professional.

- You have to be able to stand being hated or at the very least disliked by your adolescent from time to time. If you cannot, you are in for a really rough ride. No one enjoys being disliked, particularly under their own roof, but the extreme emotions to which parenthood habitually gives rise – from love to hate and everything in between – have to be safely explored, acknowledged, understood and dealt with in order for the parent–child relationship to survive its slings and arrows. There will invariably be moments – and quite long ones at that – or situations when your adolescent is uncontrollably angry towards you or full of hate. Your capacity to stand firm in the face of it is worth its weight in psychological gold. However, the reverse is also true: not being able to withstand your adolescent's anger and doing everything in your power to deflect these feelings – going back on your word, spoiling them, bribing, bargaining, pleading, cajoling, trying to buy them out of their furies, attempting to ingratiate yourself when you should be taking control – are at the very root of the many emotional problems adolescents bring to the consulting room.

- You need to know the difference between behaviours that are thoughtless or impulsive and those that are premeditated. Most transgressions by adolescents are thoughtless and impulsive. This is what adolescents are, by definition. We hope that, through experience and with our careful attention to the bigger picture, this impulsivity will lessen and they will eventually make more thoughtful, adult decisions. They may be 'guilty' but their misdemeanours might more justly be termed 'crimes of passion' than 'malice aforethought'.

As such, even though the incidents themselves may be quite shocking, they are not worth too much parental soul-searching and disproportionate angst. Most adolescents know when they have messed up although they may not openly acknowledge the fact, so there is not much to be gained from rubbing salt into the wound.

What do need special attention are those transgressions we deem to be premeditated. This is because, in order to commit them, the adolescent has to do a Faustian deal with his conscience. He or she will have thought through the consequences of their actions, at least to some extent. They will have had to temporarily silence or bypass their conscience in order to be prepared to go ahead despite knowing the chosen deed is wrong. This is more serious because the psychology is more complex. These premeditated acts are often the result of the adolescent harbouring a grievance, which is unacknowledged. The price he pays for 'righting' some unspecified injustice is high. Though he may have been able to evade his conscience in the short term, the 'feeling bad' always manifests itself eventually, invariably accompanied by self-loathing and shame. Over time, this has a deleterious effect on the adolescent's sense of worth. Punishments are appropriate up to a point, but as parents you must delve a little deeper. Something more profound is going on inside the teenager that no punishment on its own can resolve.

Harboured grievances are dangerous and I mean dangerous. The inevitable slights of life provide fuel for the notion that the world is either unfair or is 'out to get me'. This will undermine adult life in a serious way.

The best example of this is the thorny issue of stealing. It is one of those issues which has us in a lather from the outset. It's criminal, it's delinquent, people go to prison for stealing. If we can put aside the understandable moral outrage for a moment let's try and unravel the act. Most teens have stolen something or other, whether from Dad's wallet or the local store, and mostly it's a one-off. It's a crime of passion as I have outlined above: 'I want something, I take, I don't think about it.' The scale of the theft doesn't really matter in a sense. (I'm excluding bank robberies here!) Usually the theft is obvious and more often than not is detected pretty quickly.

Compare this to the teen who takes a pound or two from Mum's purse over a long period. This is much more serious. It's premeditated; each and every act has to bypass the teen's conscience. The internal workings of how they do this goes something like this: they know it's wrong but feel a 'perceived injustice', such as Mum and Dad favouring a sibling, legitimises the theft. In other words they feel they are righting a wrong. When you tackle a teenager who has impulsively taken something you will often get an outpouring of remorse but the opposite happens with the premeditated thieves. They will deny they have done it even when faced with overwhelming evidence to the contrary and will often feel very little remorse. If you suspect that this is an issue for your teenager get professional help. The perceived grievance is not immediately obvious and needs a lot of skilled work to get to the bottom of.

How Not to Punish Your Teen

It might be helpful at this point to look at some of the things we should try to avoid doing as parents.

Bullying and threatening behaviours

The most obvious and damaging response to 'bad' behaviour is to bully and threaten your teen. Sometimes this arises as a result of the parent having been bullied by their parents as a teenager, but more often it is a response to feeling impotent in the face of a truculent adolescent. The father (it's usually the father) feels he is losing his authority and responds with threatening behaviours. This is very damaging.

Moral outrage

Moral outrage is a more familiar parental response. The idea is to convey shock, horror and disbelief to your teenager, making them feel very small and/or humiliated. (In effect moral outrage has replaced the smack.) Humiliating your teenager doesn't do any good. It makes them feel resentful at best or hateful towards themselves at worst.

Being mates

Your job as a parent is to guide your child through the difficult stage of being a teenager. It is not to be their best mate or best friend. If you're busy being their friend, who is doing the parenting?

Wait and see

Many parents choose a 'wait and see' approach to teenagers. The argument goes that they will learn from their mistakes, maturity will kick in and all will sort itself out in the long run. It's a Russian roulette way of parenting and parents need to answer the following question truthfully: Is this a strategy you truly believe in or is it a default option because you want to avoid upsets and arguments? In my experience wait and see is usually a cop out.

The negotiated settlement

A popular parenting style favoured by many parents of a more democratic mindset is the negotiated settlement. This is the one in which we negotiate interim positions with our teenagers. It has all the hallmarks of a sensible adult discussion, except of course it's not with an adult, which is exactly why it doesn't work. We feel we are being terribly civilised by adopting this kind of style not realising that we are in fact engaging in a sophisticated arm-wrestle.

Negotiating the position of the goalposts is a familiar adolescent tactic. What it means in practice is that they cannot or do not want to face reality, all of which is perfectly normal for this age group. However, during this period of their life reality closes in quickly. The academic and social demands made on them are challenging and there is only minimal room for manoeuvre. If you opt for negotiated settlements you are perpetuating their childish illusion that adult life is an endless series of negotiations and fudges and the shit never really hits the fan. Negotiated settlements don't tackle problems; they fudge them.

How to Handle Punishment

First, it is important to try to shift the debate from, 'Do what I tell you', which always just disintegrates into a power struggle that you are bound to lose. Instead you need to concentrate on consequences, because consequences focus the adolescent mind like nothing else. Why? Well, they are a reality check and, if adolescence is nothing else, it is an exercise in avoiding reality checks. These irritants smack of responsibility and responsibility, to most adolescents, is something to be avoided as urgently as having a parent take to the dance floor. They are not adults yet and the pull of a more childish world without consequences is very strong. If you want to grab their attention, drop the outrage and talk about consequences. Consequences are the harder edge of life – sometimes they really hurt and of course make teenagers feel distinctly 'unhappy', for which read thwarted, frustrated and angry. Often we as parents back off and recoil from consequences too because we know they are going to create a conflict, an argument, a shouting match.

The 'two Ms' are where we start: money and mobile phone. Without either, the adolescent is effectively grounded and issues of where he goes and who he or she is with become irrelevant. If you can control the sanctions then you can control the strategy.

Returning to the story of Jonny at the beginning of the chapter, we can start by making strides onto firmer ground. One of the developmental tasks in which Jonny is engaged is attempting to gain some (psychological and emotional) distance from his parents. He can then make his own decisions, think his own thoughts and develop his own ideas. This is a work in progress and it is not linear; even if Jonny does think in a straight line, he believes he can pull it off in one go. He is going out with his friends a lot of the time, but doesn't see why there should be any need to keep his parents abreast of who he is seeing and what they are up to. He, like most teenagers, isn't overly troubled by what his parents think about his decisions, and is even less so if what they think is negative. He has his own internal logic, which is essentially at the service of what he wants to do, and very efficient it is too.

The deal for Jonny is this: he has a choice. If he wants to go out then he has to tell his parents where he is going and whom he is with. If he chooses not to, then his parents will stop his allowance and take away his mobile phone. It is up to him. Seeing it written down here, it would seem relatively easy to put in place, but I realise it is not. This is the paradox of parenting issues: it is usually fairly easy to know what to do; it is the doing of it which is the problem.

Jonny's response is likely to be explosive and unpleasant, and adolescent explosions can be frightening as well as wearing. He may say he doesn't care and follow this up with a very long rant designed to make his parents rise with the aim of drawing them into a full-blown fight.

Do not be fazed by any appearance your child may convey of not caring about having the two Ms withdrawn. Believe me, it hurts them, and badly. An adolescent without a phone is like a blind man without a stick. Without money they are severely handicapped, despite the fact that some of their friends may help out. This will only be in the short term and the paralysis over time is debilitating. Some teenagers might have a Saturday job, and therefore money of their own, so what do we do about that? The answer is to factor it in and make the ban longer. Most adolescents don't have the stomach or the character for a long war. Remember, while they are so artfully digging in with their strategy of 'not caring', their world of friends, parties and adventures is moving on apace, and they are missing out: a situation that for them is untenable.

If you can weather the storm without too much compromising, then you are more than halfway there. Sure enough your adolescent will come back with a deal, a sort of halfway house. Or he will agree to the deal and ignore it. It is now critical that you do what you say you will. No long monologue, just consequences. Do not back down or do deals. You will get no thanks for being reasonable. You will merely be laying the foundations for further protracted disputes.

So what does this look like in practice? Choose your time, sit your child down and tell him what's going to happen. Sit back and listen to the diatribe/rant that will follow. Nod your head as if you fully understand the validity of his thoughts but quietly tell him that unfortunately this is the deal and it's a 'take it or leave it' deal. Most teenagers will use that moment to create a diversion, often by storming off. That, in their mind, effectively ends the story. It's one of those teenage tactics that gives them a feeling that they have erased the last hour of their life. An alternative reaction is for him to say that he doesn't care and you can do what you want. This is a bluff. You just need to hold your nerve. Whatever you do don't go back to the debate and try and reinforce it with further explanations. You are just offering another opportunity for your teen to wind you or himself up. Adolescents like nothing better than an inconclusive row and one that doesn't involve consequences is even better.

Sophie is 14 but looks 16 and thinks she's 18. She's tall, attractive, confident and feisty. She is already launching herself into adolescent life as if she's a skydiver jumping from a plane. Her friends and social life are the main things in her life. She wants to be out all the time, even during the week. Her parents have come to see me to discuss how much leeway to give her and what kind of boundaries to put down. They can't agree on a curfew or on what sort of social events she should be allowed to go to and those she shouldn't. I can see their point; it's not black and white. In truth the meeting is a distraction. It is fairly clear that this parental discussion is academic: the reality is that Sophie does exactly what she wants and, as far as I can tell, the basis of her parents' decision-making is how much energy they have to argue with Sophie and/or how much of a fuss Sophie kicks up. This is familiar ground for all of us. The question becomes not so much how much leeway to give Sophie but, more, how to gain some control over her burgeoning social life. This situation is more complicated because once you've conceded ground to an adolescent it is very difficult to haul any back. Someone like Sophie is going to come out all guns blazing if her parents start trying to curtail her.

There is, though, an aspect of adolescent behaviour that works to our advantage as parents. Their rants and tempers, however erudite and cutting, are just hot air. 'No, you can't,' may be followed by an hour's diatribe on the injustices of the world but, once they have vented, threatened and pleaded, they will stop. The adolescent world moves on very quickly. The golden rule is to listen, but don't attempt to proffer counterarguments. Counterarguments are like petrol on a fire. Acknowledge that you've heard her views but that the boundary still stands. Counterarguments are pointless because the Sophies of this world are engaged in a monologue. Dialogue has yet to be discovered.

Our first meeting as a family is quite something. Sophie is agitated but up for the fight. Perfectly logically, she asks why they want to put the brakes on her social life now, when previously they didn't bother. Dad puts forward his eloquent and well-argued case for the defence. He is both calm and reasonable. As I listen to this I have to remind myself that we are talking to a 14-year-old, we are not in a business meeting. I know what Dad is thinking. He believes that eventually Sophie will bow to his superior logic. Sophie listens, she's a bright girl and I can see she is finding his logic difficult to rebut and his reasonableness appealing. She's smart enough to know he's right. Unfortunately, we're not having an abstract discussion; we are having an arm-wrestle about adolescent freedom. For Sophie the stakes are high; for her it feels like life or death. Three-quarters of the way through her father's case for the defence, I notice Sophie has switched off and is gearing herself up for an assault. She is furiously running her fingers through her hair.

She starts with the social exclusion argument. The one that goes, 'None of my friends have curfews and rules' (untrue but oddly persuasive). She then moves up a gear to the character assassination laced with guilt: 'You are both hypocrites. First you do one thing and then you change your mind. Why do you care about curfews now? Is it his idea [looking at me]? You two are out every Saturday with your friends. What am I supposed to do? Stay in my room all night?'

She is working herself up and I can see her parents starting to become anxious. I jump in to help them.

'Sophie, there are going to be curfews and rules because you are 14, so that's not up for discussion, but there is a bit of give round the edges.'

This has backed Sophie into a corner and doesn't go down well at all; she's spitting blood.

'I'm not agreeing to anything,' she counters. 'I can do what I want. You can't stop me.'

'I take that to mean you're leaving all the decisions to us, have I got that right?' I say.

'I'm not listening to this rubbish,' she yells, and storms out of the room.

Her parents look on rather awkwardly and apologise profusely for Sophie's behaviour, these sorts of public outbursts are difficult to take as a parent. Parenting adolescents is exhausting and extremely testing. It tests our patience but, more importantly, it tests our stamina and our character. We sit in silence for a moment and her father asks me what we should do now. I am clear that we sit and wait it out. I am fairly confident that Sophie will come back. She has played her ace card but nothing has really been resolved. This particular act in the drama has ended and my guess is that she won't want us to be talking about her behind her back. Ten minutes later Sophie walks back in as calm as you like, but still protesting that she's not negotiating. I can see she's taken aback by the fact that we haven't capitulated. She doesn't quite know where to go with it. Eventually we get down to a reasonable but pointless discussion about boundaries.

Over the next few months we have all-out war. Sophie's parents and I agree what sort of boundaries she needs and the options available to us if she doesn't cooperate. That is the simple bit. But the 'doing' proves problematic. Her parents don't really believe it will work and Sophie knows it. She seizes upon these moments of doubt and drives a truck full speed straight through the road block.

It all comes to a head when Sophie goes missing for the whole weekend having agreed to Friday evening out only. She arrives back late Sunday night looking exhausted and dishevelled. Her phone battery had died sometime on Saturday, apparently, which is why she didn't call her parents. This popular defence always amuses me. Why do their phone batteries always run out at the weekend when they are out and why do they never borrow someone else's phone to make a call? Funny, that.

The worry and rising panic about what might have happened to her at last galvanises her parents. Dad confiscates her mobile phone indefinitely and stops her allowance. Sophie is initially too exhausted to argue but is oddly quieter in the weeks that follow. The long weekend, it transpires, had not been quite as much fun as she had hoped, in fact quite the opposite. It was never made explicit what had happened but clearly things had gone on that had worried and frightened her. Like a lot of young adolescents without adequate boundaries, Sophie had misjudged the situation and suddenly found herself out of her depth. In many respects she was lucky in as much as nothing truly grave occurred.

Here is another erroneous adolescent parenting myth: bad things only ever happen to other families' teenagers.

It didn't take Sophie long to get back on the horse. For her, the nightmare of the long weekend quickly receded and she was soon back pushing the boundaries and trying to break the rules. But the weekend nightmare had profoundly changed her parents. The panic they had experienced wondering whether they would ever see Sophie again was still fresh in their memory. It had been a huge wake-up call. They did not forget so quickly and, after it, they were able to remain more steadfast in the face of Sophie's blasts. Their steadfastness, in turn, calmed Sophie down as she realised that she was now banging her head against a brick wall. Faced with an immovable object, Sophie eventually capitulated and normal service was resumed. It is always worth sacrificing being liked by your teenager in exchange for a guarantee of their safety and long-term balance.

Sophie's story illustrates a seminal parenting issue: how to link their independence with responsibility. Unless you have a super mature teen, their idea of nirvana is likely to be total freedom without a shred of responsibility. In other words, 'I can do what I want and you can't stop me.' This sort of challenge has the potential to draw parents into one of those pointless wrestling matches. Remember, focus on the consequences for their actions and ditch the monologues.

Where to Draw the Line

This is one of those parental discussions that can last for years. In my experience a decision is usually made on the basis of how tired we are and/or how much the adolescent pushes. However, what it should be based on is whether an activity is appropriate or not, and this is a more difficult issue especially for the younger adolescent. They often feel your doubts and questions are unnecessary, intrusive and infantilising. They dramatically accuse you of being overprotective or even of 'stalking' them. Do not buy into this. The younger adolescent is prone to exaggerate their competence and maturity.

The main issue to keep in mind here is their safety. In my view, it is perfectly reasonable to want to know where they are going and, for example, to determine whether a parent will be around when they go on a sleepover. It will be a very different sleepover if the older brother or sister is in charge as opposed to if a parent is monitoring it. You might want to know whether alcohol will be allowed. You would be surprised by how smart teenagers are at sneaking alcohol into what might seem like a simple sleepover. You might also want to be clear whether it is a coed sleepover and, if so, whether boys and girls will be sleeping in separate rooms. These are perfectly legitimate questions. It is my view that these issues are non-negotiable for the younger adolescent. By and large they are not experienced enough or knowledgeable enough about themselves for negotiation to be a worthwhile and productive strategy. Don't get seduced into deals. Disappointment doesn't last long in the teenage mind.

The deal is different and more complex for older adolescents but, again, your guiding principle is the extent to which they successfully link responsibility to independence. Because they are older and their social life plays a much bigger part in their life, the discussions about what is and is not allowed can be intense and exchanges can become heated. A 'no' to an important social event can feel like a death sentence to a teen. However, the strength of their 'pleading' shouldn't be a factor in your decision-making. When making a decision, ask yourself the following questions:

- Is the event appropriate?
- Can they be trusted to behave safely and appropriately?
- Do I know any of the other teenagers who will be going?

Curfews

The curfew problem for older adolescents has become a lot more complex over the last 10 years. It seems that events/parties start and finish much later and this presents parents with huge problems when deciding an appropriate time for their teen to be home. I think it's worth shifting the debate away from time (usually decided randomly by parents) to safety. The later your teen is out the more likely they are at risk because of drinking. If they are under the influence of alcohol they are likely to make poorer judgements and the normal fantasy of adolescent indestructibility increases. It may be more productive to focus on how they will get home safely and with whom rather than fixate on the time. However worried we may be as parents, it is not a solution to lock our teens up and throw away the key. You have to make a risk assessment. What I would say is that to err on the cautious side is not being overprotective.

The reason I say this is not out of some reverence for old-fashioned values. It's more to do with how psychologically valuable conflict is. All the time spent arguing about boundaries keeps the issue at the forefront of the teenager's mind and this is important when they are out and about. In psychology speak you are 'trying' to engage their executive function, the area that makes reasoned decisions.

The conditional deal

At this stage of an adolescent's development the (unspoken) deal between parents and child should go something like this: 'We will support you in whatever you do provided that you are keeping up your end of the deal, and that means putting in your best effort at school and behaving responsibly socially.' This means sticking to the deal they make. This should be a conditional not an unconditional deal. The unconditional deal – 'We will love you whatever you do' – belongs to the younger child.

What does a conditional deal mean in practice? It means there are consequences to actions. Now I know this is incredibly difficult to see through in practice. You are faced with concerns such as: 'What do we do if he just packs his bags and flounces out?' 'What if he threatens to leave school?' 'What if he gets violent?' In many situations these are all legitimate concerns, but I would suggest that such threats are merely a reflection of his/her fear of facing up to the demands of the adult world. It is better to deal with these issues now, when there is still everything to play for, than muddle through in the hope that the penny will eventually drop.

There are some practical steps you can take at this stage if you feel things are going off the rails:

- You need a plan. If you spend your time randomly fire-fighting it is much easier to lose sight of what you are trying to achieve. You need a strategy for dealing with their social life and their school life. You need to have some clarity about what you expect from them behaviourally towards you, and their siblings if they have any. You need to be available to talk.
- Tackle the problem head-on – no fudges or deals.
- Don't fall for the old myth that 'they will grow out of it' as justification for doing nothing. It is never quite clear how

this 'growing out of it' is going to come about. The nub of this argument is that maturational processes kick in and whatever the problem is it resolves itself in time. The trouble is, most of us have no clear idea of how these convenient maturational processes will take the child forward or when they will, just that they will, eventually. It is true that superficially it can look as if maturation has moved things on. In my experience, what appears to be a resolution is in fact a mutation. By this I mean that when the adolescent is nudging into her late teens or early twenties, she may appear in her 'maturity' to have overcome the problem, but in fact has only managed to cover it up or navigate her way round it by manipulating her behaviour, and this is not a good basis on which to enter full-blown adulthood. A much more pertinent question to ask is what happens if they don't grow out of it? If you ask this question you have already started making a contingency plan.

When Things Go Too Far

Disruptive behaviour

The majority of adolescents will have endured the odd detention or two during a long school career. Growing up is a tricky business but there are the serial offenders, those adolescents who seem to be permanently in trouble. They are, to all intents and purposes, impervious to sanctions and yet, so often when talking about these difficult pupils, teachers temper their frustration with comments along the lines of, despite being pains in the neck, these children are engaging and good-hearted. What might be going on and what might we do about them?

Serial offending has a complex structure. Children can often appear cocky and display a cavalier attitude to authority but this invariably covers up a basic lack of confidence, a deep insecurity and/or a need to control the group.

Jacob is 13. He is a skinny little chap with a head that looks too large for his body owing to his mass of curly hair. He's a dead ringer for sixties pop star, Marc Bolan. He is popular at school with staff and other pupils but his school is becoming fed up with the amount of time his errant behaviour is taking up. He seems to have commandeered the role of class clown and never misses an opportunity to try to make his classmates laugh. He has been spoken to ad infinitum by the teachers and has had numerous detentions but all to no effect. Jacob bounces into the consulting room and greets me like a long-lost friend. My first impression of Jacob is of a cheerful, confident young boy. He is chatty, funny and engaging. He loves coming to see me. He has my undivided attention and for Jacob that's perfect. Initially it is hard to reconcile my first impression with his reputation as a serial troublemaker.

Over the coming weeks, though, I see a very different picture emerging. Jacob is desperate for my attention and his efforts to entertain me are too persistent. He is like a much younger child jumping up and down in front of an adult as if to say, 'Look at me!' The trouble is, he is thirteen and not three. The second pattern I note is that he wants me to like him and tries hard to entertain me with his stories and joke-telling. His desperation to be liked is painful to watch. It is as though he is not in control of himself and the desperate behaviour takes over. As the weeks go by, I am more able to see evidence of a lack of confidence and an insecure sense of self, allied to a need to monopolise adult attention. He doesn't think he is very smart. He would like to be in the school football team but he is not good enough to get into the first eleven. He is about to enter adolescence and feels anxious that he is just not good enough to make a mark. His serial offending has also become a sort of self-fulfilling prophecy: the more he does it, the more it is expected of him and he expects it of himself.

With these kinds of adolescents there is often a perceived deprivation, real or imagined, which has to be addressed. The key is not to give the adolescent more attention, especially negative attention. Jacob needs to find something – an activity or challenge – that will reward him with a feeling of real achievement. The attention he gets from this will be all-important positive attention, as opposed to the eviscerating negative attention to which he has become too accustomed.

His parents' account of Jacob's life is fairly normal except for his reaction to his brother's birth. It seems he was badly affected by the arrival of a sibling, as many children are. According to his parents this is when his attention-seeking behaviour started. One might reasonably speculate that the grievance was the birth of his brother. His parents get the picture immediately and they sign him up for a number of activities that we hope will boost his self-esteem and confidence. Importantly, they insist he has to stick with them; in other words, he cannot opt out. The activities are challenging and initially Jacob is a reluctant participant. He tries to persuade his father to let him drop them but his father makes him stick at it. Over the coming months Jacob's disruptive behaviour lessens and his school detentions diminish. What becomes apparent in the consulting room is a marked lessening of his irritating stories and jokes. He appears more settled in himself and without the desperation he is much easier to be with. Within a few months Jacob has become part of the school community. He has remained a much more confident young man and should be okay going forward.

All adolescents are insecure; although it is true that some are more insecure than others. What gives them confidence and security is experience and achievements (in the broadest sense). So if you have an adolescent who is constantly in trouble you have to understand that this is a compensatory behaviour. Try to get him or her into something that gives them a good feeling about themselves. It doesn't have to be anything particularly grand – choir or a sports team are fine. If they are reluctant it is usually because they feel they won't succeed at it. Fear of failing is a huge issue for adolescents, especially those who are disruptive. You will have to help them get over this by talking it through. They may ignore you, they may create a scene, but try to stick with it. It doesn't matter if you lose the odd skirmish. Concentrate on the long game instead. It's a game that adolescents don't play very well. Simple though this sounds, most parents, particularly fathers, find this incredibly difficult. They cannot stand to have their authority challenged and end up fighting from positions of weakness. Many parents don't want to use 'strategy' at all, so they end up fighting on the adolescent's terms and wonder why they have no control.

The impossible adolescent

I frequently receive calls from exasperated parents; their adolescent son or daughter just doesn't seem to respond to any of their requests to adhere to boundaries. They appear, superficially at least, reckless, confident and wilful. Punishments don't make any difference; they are a law unto themselves and won't listen to anyone. Their behaviour is out of control.

> Sixteen-year-old Robert comes with a reputation and history that suggests he's heading not only for expulsion but possibly prison. His mother has had enough. She gave up trying to manage him some while ago. He attends school sporadically and spends most of his time with an unsavoury group of teenagers who flirt with serious

trouble. In my experience it is only a matter of time before he finds himself in deep water. He has one big supporter though, his art teacher. Robert is good at art, and he and the teacher have struck up a positive relationship. He has persuaded Robert to come and see me at the clinic. Quite how the man pulled off this feat, I don't know. Robert is a big, powerful lad for his age. His physicality is imposing and he knows it. Although he is white he speaks in a London patois, a mix of Afro-Caribbean and cockney, and he is wearing the trademark baseball cap.

He opens our meeting with a challenge. He tells me his art teacher wanted him to come but he reckons it's a waste of time.

'I don't give a fuck what you think or anybody else.'

With adolescents like Robert you usually only have one chance to make a connection. You have to pitch it right. If you are too friendly or too distant it will fail. However, the fact that he's come at all is positive even with the disclaimer that he doesn't care. There is also his relationship with the art teacher, which is a good sign.

While his opening comment is a sort of threat, it also contains a lot of information about his state of mind. It is a coded statement about his self-worth. What he is saying is: if I don't care about anything, then nothing can hurt or disappoint me. It is a sort of insurance policy against the vicissitudes of relationships. Turned the other way round, he is saying how much he has been hurt and that he can't take any more. His physicality and threatening manner is his defence against intimacy. This is a familiar gambit for impossible adolescents. They create an atmosphere of hopelessness or intimidation, which envelops them and all those around them. The key to working with them is not to become caught up in it but to focus on what it is disguising.

'Why don't we do a deal?' I say. 'Let's see how this meeting goes and, if it's useless, we'll call it quits and leave it. If we feel we get somewhere, let's make another time.'

He is quiet for a minute as he thinks about my offer. I have handed over control of the meetings to him. He agrees.

'I've read the notes, Robert. Not good reading is it?' (I'm referring to all his scrapes and misdemeanours, written by sundry teachers and social workers.)

He shrugs his shoulders in a 'couldn't care less' manner.

'What happened to your father?' I ask. 'It says [referring to my notes] he's not around but doesn't mention what happened to him.'

Robert sits bolt upright in his chair.

'Why do you want to know?'

'It's important, isn't it, you know, what happened to him? It doesn't say anything in the notes. I'm curious.'

Robert looks extremely uncomfortable. There is a tense atmosphere between us. I can sense he's grappling with a dilemma. If he starts talking about his father, the chances are he will feel upset and his vulnerability will be all too evident. We don't have the requisite trust between us for this to be safe, far from it. I am still a figure of some suspicion. He might end up feeling ashamed or humiliated.

That would be the end of any chance of further work. I decide to help him out.

'Look, let's leave it for another time.'

He looks mightily relieved.

The rest of the meeting is low-key and devoid of any meaningful contact between us. We talk about trivia, football and music, but it doesn't matter. His cover is blown, so to speak. He has revealed his vulnerability. He knows I have seen it. He cares a great deal about his absent father.

Our meetings are sporadic over the coming months. He attends one week and then misses the next two. He is forever testing whether I will give up on him. We stick with it for the best part of a year, which I considered an achievement in itself. It would be untrue to claim that Robert made a huge amount of progress, but he did start attending school on a more regular basis and managed to pass some GCSEs.

Robert had had a close relationship with his father but, when Robert was seven, his father walked out on the family and was never seen again. Robert didn't know whether he was alive or dead. This loss had had a traumatic effect on his life. All these years later he could barely speak about it without tears. At those moments, the intimidating, surly adolescent gave way to a weeping, abandoned little boy. How our meetings came to an end was to be expected in the light of Robert's history. At some point in therapy, life-changing events are nearly always re-enacted in some way between patient and analyst. Robert eventually abandoned me. He stopped coming without warning. No text, no call, he just disappeared. I kept his appointment time free for many weeks in the hope he would show up again. I wrote and tried to contact him but he and his mother had moved. I never heard from him again. I don't think we did enough work for any major transformation to have taken place, but I can only hope that we had done enough for him not to repeat the pattern with his own family in the future.

With impossible adolescents you have to understand a crucial point and it is this: their behaviour is the symptom and not the cause, so, unless you engage with the cause, all your efforts to sort out the behaviour will come to nothing. So what might be behind this sort of acting out? Although it may not appear so, there is no question that this kind of adolescent is desperate. These teenagers have somehow silenced or become temporarily detached from the part of themselves that mediates their behaviour and keeps them safe. They are in a kind of deluded state, a world that appears to have no consequences. Forget all their surface cool and apparent indifference; it is all bravado. Beneath the apparent lawlessness lies fear, sometimes terror and very often despair.

But fear of what? Living through adolescence is a painful experience and it involves a lot of suffering; the suffering involved in not being in control of one's life or emotions; of feeling weak and helpless at times; the fear that you might never be able to manage without your parents. These are just some of the numerous concerns of teens. What better way to get round these fears than by morphing into a 'couldn't care less', out-of-control adolescent? Looking for all the world as fearless as can be is a marvellous way, or so they imagine, of deflecting the reality, which is that they are petrified. In short, the more impossible the adolescent, the more fearful they are.

If you can make sense of what I have just written then it makes it much easier to deal with your impossible adolescent son or daughter because you will be able to see through the carapace and not be intimidated by their apparent 'impossibility'. If you focus on what underpins this 'impossibility', you will be much more effective at your job. In order to do this you have to try and address the hopelessness and crippling fear that underpins their behaviour by talking to them. This is not easy either for them or for you. Remember that one of the central issues for teenagers is the belief that they will never have to confront 'reality', so denial is a huge part of their armoury. Name these fears and don't be put off if you don't get a positive response. Try not to resort to draconian punishments – they are meat and drink to these sorts of teenagers because at heart they don't much care for themselves. If they won't open up to you then it might be useful to bring in a professional. If they baulk at that suggestion, as many do, try and get them to give it a go just once.

The impossible adolescent needs to be reeled in slowly and this will take time – weeks and, in extreme cases, months – so you need to be persistent. Try and avoid becoming drawn into pointless wars that serve as a smoke-screen to distract you from what is really concerning them. They will try to make you feel hopeless and it can be a real test of your fortitude as a parent. It will, in fact, be a relief for them to know that you are not taken in by their bravado and that you do understand what they are really concerned about. It is possible they will collapse in a heap, but it is more likely that they will simply dismiss your comments as rubbish primarily to save face. Don't expect gratitude for your careful handling of the situation.

Don't worry, your voice will have been heard. Somewhere inside them, they will be relieved that you are not fooled by their outrageous antics and that you know why they are struggling.

Top Tips

- **Make decisions based on how well your teenager is able to link freedom with responsibility not on what others are doing or how big the event is.**
- **Don't fret about losing the odd skirmish, we all do.** You have plenty of time to deal with the incident later on.
- **Remember that acting out behaviour is a symptom not a cause.** You have to understand what it is that is driving your teen's behaviour. It's usually insecurity, low self-esteem or separation anxiety.

- **Whatever you do don't use the excuse that 'they will grow out of it' as a recipe for doing nothing.**
- **Try to avoid getting caught in 'persuasive' discussions.**
  You will either lose or it will end up in a row.
- **If you have an 'impossible' adolescent you are going to have to take some time to sort out what the real problem is and what sort of strategy to use.**
  It's a big project and you might benefit from some professional help to see the project through.

The vast majority of teenage 'crimes' are a result of immaturity and thoughtlessness – by all means be firm and concerned but don't rub their noses in it; most are insecure enough as it is. Although it won't necessarily be evident their conscience will give them a hard enough time.

CHAPTER 6

Relationships

Helping teenagers to develop the capacity to create and sustain meaningful relationships is one of the central tenets of this book. If you need proof of the importance of developing and sustaining relationships, the Grant Study provides it. Set up in the late 1930s by store magnate W T Grant, the study followed the path of 268 Harvard students over a 70-year period, looking at their physical and emotional life. The Grant Study essentially asked the question, 'What is it that keeps us happy and healthy?' The study's key findings are:

1. Social connections are good for our mental and physical health.
2. It's not the number of connections but the quality of the relationships that matter.
3. Good relationships protect the brain and body as we get older.

Looked at the other way round, isolation, loneliness and the inability to make deep and lasting relationships with partners and friends lead to mental and physical problems.

The capacity to make deep and meaningful relationships with partners and friends is a far more important indicator of well-being than wealth, education, class or status, which is why it is so important that, as parents, we help our teens to foster and sustain positive friendships.

But the tricky question is, how do we do this? To a large extent children arrive at adolescence with an existing template, a result of the kind of relationships they have forged in the family with parents and siblings plus their own friendship DNA. Some children are inherently more sociable and more skilled at relationships than others. Whatever template your teen arrives with will be severely tested by three separate developments:

1. Hormonal changes.
2. The difference in the structure of teenage relationships (I answer this a few lines down).
3. The capricious nature of the adolescent group.

Hormonal changes, which impact on mind and body, cause the teen to become preoccupied with self. You can call it selfishness if you like, but it is a necessary preoccupation, as in 'I need to understand what is going on inside me.' This preoccupation is more often than not accompanied by acute self-consciousness. These changes can have a significant impact on self-esteem. The once confident 11-year-old is now all at sea in this new version of herself. Spots may appear randomly, and teenage acne can crucify self-esteem. Whatever form this biological change takes it will impact on your teen's relationships. If the changes are unwelcome then self-confidence goes out of the window and self-consciousness goes through the roof. Your teen needs you on hand to continually provide positive reinforcement and listen attentively to their anxieties, however trivial they might seem. Pay attention to the cause of your teen's insecurity and anxiety. This can often take a bit of digging around, but when you eventually get to the bottom of the issue, don't trivialise it or mock it. It is easy to poke fun at teenage anxieties because they can seem much ado about nothing, but that's not how it feels in the world of the adolescent. In their world it's often all-consuming. Make sure your teen doesn't withdraw or drop out of clubs and activities at this stage. It is so important to reinforce the truth that every one of their friends is dealing with the same thing.

As they start to dip their toes in the world of friendships outside the home your teen will quickly learn that the home template has to be adapted. Home relationships are by and large unconditional. You love your child whatever they do. This isn't so outside of the family group. Friendships are conditional. In other words, there is a deal between friends. You cannot expect your friend to stay your friend if you treat them badly. Some adolescents get this more quickly than others, but it isn't automatic and you need to be on hand to help them make the transition. A judicious comment suggesting your son's friend Charlie might welcome a call as his grandmother died is the kind of thing I am getting at. Or a suggestion that your daughter calls her friend Emily, who is always the one to call your daughter and must be getting fed up of doing so. These sorts of actions appear obvious to us, but they can bypass the young teen who is spending an inordinate amount of time in the bathroom obsessing about her fringe or deciding which side he should part his hair.

The young adolescent group has all the stability of a bamboo hut in a hurricane. To survive and flourish in these groups adolescents need to be able to share, to take turns, have a capacity to empathise, a degree of self-confidence and a lot of resilience. That is quite a checklist! Not many teens have all those attributes in their locker and consequently they are all vulnerable to some extent and need you on hand to help them navigate the turbulent seas of adolescence. They don't automatically understand what is happening in the group and why a certain member is acting in such a way. Making sense of it for them and explaining certain behaviours is crucial. You are giving them the tools to survive and flourish in a difficult and complex environment.

How to Nurture Teenage Relationships

Alison's parents have come to see me. She is 13 and has suddenly started having problems with her friends. It has become so bad that she has been refusing to go to school and is pestering her parents to move her. Her parents are unsure what to do. They are also perplexed as to what is going on. Alison has always made friends easily and is confident and very sociable. It transpires a new girl has joined the school and the friends in Alison's group have decamped to a new group. To make matters worse, this new girl has taken against Alison and has orchestrated a campaign to exclude her from the group. At least this is Alison's explanation.

However, when I dig deeper the picture looks a little different. Alison has younger twin sisters. According to her parents they get on well, although Alison is very bossy and controlling. She is forever telling them what to do and what not to do. She has to be reminded that she is not their parent. I ask about whether she is the same with her friends. They are not sure but suspect from what they have heard that it is the same.

Alison has arrived at adolescence with a template, which is that she has to be in charge of the group. Alison has assumed that role in her small group of friends. What has happened in effect is a sort of coup d'état. The new girl has effectively deposed Alison.

This analysis helps us understand what we as parents need to do. Firstly, moving schools will not solve the problem, as Alison will likely do the same thing in the next group. Instead she needs help understanding what has gone wrong and how she needs to alter her behaviour accordingly. This starts in the home by helping Alison find better ways to be part of the family. She needs to be helped to find an alternative, more positive way to relate at home by bringing to her attention the behaviours which are causing the problem. How you deliver these messages is almost as important as the message itself. If you deliver it in a critical way it will be rejected. You have to be positive when you see attempts to change. She also needs to get back to school. These early adolescent groups are very transient and it won't be problematic to find another group, it will just take a little time.

Alison's story is relatively common and straightforward but this isn't always the case. If your teen is too competitive, not good at empathising and as a consequence is having trouble with friends, then you have to engage in lengthier dialogues:

'What do you think he felt when he got left out?'
'Do you think they get fed up with you always having to win?'
'Do you think Sam likes being the butt of all the jokes?'

These are examples of how to open the dialogue. Often your teen's response will be of the 'I didn't think of that' kind. Having planted the seed you can continue to go back to it. For example, you might ask how Sam is doing or pose a more general question about how he/she is getting on in the group. You are, in effect, educating your teen, but it takes time and a lot of conversations.

It is part of the rite of passage that accompanies teenage groups that there is frequently a massive fall out between friends. The tensions involved in being part of the group or a friendship inevitably explode at some point. It can feel cataclysmic and irreparable to the teen and that's where we as parents come in. They often don't have the tools or the confidence to heal the split and it requires a lot of talking and strategising to get it fixed. Try not to resort to blithe clichés like 'It will be all right' and leave them to it. You need to get in there and help them fix it. Be specific to the point of telling them exactly what they need to do to fix it.

Dealing with withdrawal

Sometimes the situation is more serious. This usually involves a gradual withdrawal from peer group involvement. Spending too much time in their bedroom and isolation at school are signs that development has stalled. Don't ignore it and use the argument that 'She seems perfectly happy on her own' as an excuse for doing nothing. This may be so in the short term but you can't get through adolescence successfully without some level of engagement with others.

Withdrawal has several causes. Sometimes it involves an omnipotent fantasy of the 'I don't need anyone' kind. It can be a result of not knowing how to be in the group. It can also be a terrible fear of rejection or a fear of being humiliated. Whatever it is get on to it. Don't allow your child to spend hours on their own in their bedroom. Try to get them engaged with the world via a collective activity such as cycling, singing, swimming, acting: anything that makes them have to engage with others. Try to get to the bottom of why they are withdrawing from contact. This takes time and a certain finessing of the dialogue. A heavy-handed approach won't work and will most likely only reinforce the problem. If you can't make any headway, then seek the help of a professional.

I repeat, whatever you do don't ignore it.

Top Tips

- **Do they have friends and do they seem to rub along reasonably well with them?**
  If not you have to intervene and find out why.
- **Is the family template working reasonably well in the group or not?**
- **Don't be frigtened to intervene to help fix fractures between friends.** Sometimes they don't know how to do it.
- **'Withdrawal' can have serious repercussions – get to the bottom of it.**

It is not enough to just log that your teen does or doesn't have friends; most do. You need to broaden their understanding of how relationships work. Unlike much of parenting work with teenagers, you will have a more or less captive audience when it comes to speaking about relationships. Teens are usually desperate for decent friendships and are keen to know what to say or do to nurture them.

CHAPTER 7

Sex and Pornography

Sex and adolescence are inextricably linked, if not sexual exploration then sexual thoughts. It's pervasive for all; no adolescent escapes. This is difficult work for any teenager and it takes a long time to get comfortable with this side of their life. The road to integration is perilous in today's world and needs us to be at our most sensitive and switched on to guide them through it. It is also a very private area and our efforts to discuss it with them have to be finely nuanced. Get it wrong and all hell can break loose or, of course, we could just stick our heads in the sand and pretend it's not happening.

I do understand why this might feel like the best option. We have first to get to grips with the reality of our teens as sexual beings. This is not easy. Secondly it requires us to think about our own attitudes and feelings towards sex. This could and does get complicated. Parents, by and large, are on solid ground in dealing with teenage concerns about sexual orientation. However the increasing prevalence of more complex issues about gender identity are a whole other kettle of fish. The rise in gender dysphoria (a disconnect between sex assigned at birth and an internal sense of who they are) is real enough. This subject is far too complex and far-reaching to go in to sufficient detail here – in fact it probably requires a whole other book – and I wouldn't want to gloss over anything. There are some sensible guidelines though:

1. Use the teens preferred name
2. Be your teens advocate
3. Educate yourself and get support
4. Give your teenager unconditional support.

There are many very useful websites you can go to; here are two that I particularly recommend.

www.hrc.org/trans-youth

www.mermaidsuk.org.uk

If we accept that we have to be involved in some potentially awkward and difficult conversations it is useful to give some thought to three central questions. This will help you break it down into manageable chunks.

1. When should I intervene?
2. How do I intervene?
3. What should I say?

When to intervene

As soon as the adolescent group becomes mixed or more interested in the opposite sex group is the time to intervene. And the number one topic that needs addressing is the question of relationships with the opposite sex. Try not to fall into the age-old trap of thinking that it's not on your teen's radar. Believe me, it is; directly in the sense that they are already exploring sex or indirectly in that they aren't yet exploring sex but are listening to all the stories and explanations from their friends. Most adolescent boys are already too familiar with pornography, a subject I will go into in more detail later (page 130).

How to intervene

Try to take a practical matter-of-fact approach to the basics and when talking about relationships you need to appeal to their often quite rigid sense of right and wrong. Focus on issues of respect and self-esteem towards themselves and others.

What to say

For the younger teen (I use the term 'teen' loosely here because bodily changes may take place a lot earlier than 13) this might start with some basic biology – how the changes to their body will take place and why. While this basic information is useful and only repeats what they have been told at school it is more crucial that you are on hand to debunk the various myths peddled by the school know-all. There is a mass of misinformation flying round the school playground. A familiar one from the consulting room is the myth that you can get pregnant from sitting on a toilet seat, and there are plenty more.

There needs to be real authority in your discussions about sex and relationships. This should include respect for the other, and might include sexual exploration or not. Your teen needs to understand what consent is.

> Consent requires an unequivocal 'yes'. It doesn't follow on from 'I don't know', 'I'm not sure' or 'maybe'. Consent under the influence of drugs or alcohol is a dubious area – no always means no.

They need to think about what they are comfortable with sexually and what they are not. You need to help them understand the difference between participating in sexual explorations because they feel they have to and participating because they want to. There is a huge difference between the two. Boys need to know that it isn't okay to pester or put a girl under pressure for some sort of gratification rather like ordering a takeaway.

'Friends with benefits' (casual sex without being in a relationship), casual 'hook-ups' (random encounters) and sexting all need to be on your radar. You are not going to stop these sorts of encounters, but you can explain the downsides and the effects on your teen's feelings of self-worth.

You also need to alert your teen to the dangers of engaging in sexual activity when they have drunk too much or taken drugs. Alcohol and drugs are an attractive option for teenagers because they artificially boost confidence and loosen inhibitions. However, nearly all the referrals I have had connected with adverse sexual experiences have included drugs and/or alcohol somewhere along the line.

These are all complex and difficult discussions but your teenager will have to make important decisions about these issues sooner than you think. In my experience a lot of upsetting things happen precisely because both sexes haven't been adequately prepared for them. I have no hard evidence for this view, but again it is my experience that parents are more blasé about their son's views on sex than they are about their daughter's. Boys need more help in my opinion because they are more likely to have their ideas warped by watching pornography.

Pornography

The place of pornography in society is a major issue for teenagers. It is arguably one of the most difficult and complex parenting issues that we are required to deal with. The Internet and social media have exacerbated the problem. The immediacy and speed of potential interactions mean that actions bypass thought far too easily and too often. A storm is created in the blink of an eye, almost before the teen has had time to make a thoughtful judgement about whether what they are engaging in is appropriate or not. The impact that pornography can have on our adolescent's developing sense of self and relational life is such that we have no choice but to engage with it. And here is the sting in the tail: dealing with it effectively requires us to acquaint ourselves with some of the more unexplored areas of our own sexual life and that is a tricky business.

A boy's perspective

William was nearly 16 when he came to see me because of sleeping difficulties; at least that was the presenting symptom. The cause of it was a whole other kettle of fish. He was tall, physically mature and had an air of confidence about him. He looked a lot older; he could at a pinch have got away with being 17. He was the youngest of four and I suspect had had to toughen up to hold his own.

Our first meeting was something of an exploratory affair, as we looked at what his sleeping difficulties might be about. I sensed we were skirting around an issue he wasn't quite ready to talk about. Two-thirds of the way through our meeting he suddenly dropped a bombshell. He told me he wanted to talk about pornography. He disclosed that he had been regularly watching pornography since he was 11. I was slightly taken aback. I was quite aware that watching pornography was common among teenage boys but 11 seemed to be pushing it.

'How often?' I asked.

'I reckon about six to seven hours a week. Not really sure,' he replied.

'Do your parents know?' I asked.

'No, they haven't a clue. I just say I'm going to my bedroom to do some work. They never bother to check my computer or me. I think they are relieved that I'm out of the way. They can get some peace and quiet.' Fear suddenly filtered across his face.

'You're not going to tell them are you? My mum would die if she knew and my dad would kill me.'

I reassured him that I wouldn't.

'So, let me get this right: you've been watching this stuff since you were 11?'

William had picked up my surprise and shock but it was only the beginning.

'I need to talk about other stuff that's happened, I feel really bad.'

What William revealed was disturbing but I suspect more common than we would like to imagine. He spoke of a series of sexual encounters with teenage girls driven by the pornography that he had been watching. It was arguable whether or not these encounters could be classified as sexual assaults. They were a series of 'hook-ups'; one-off incidents usually. He used the fact that the girls liked him or wanted to be liked by him to manipulate them into performing various sexual acts. Sometimes they would be drunk, sometimes not. As far as I could work out most of the girls said no to his demands, which were as upfront and explicit as you could get. Occasionally he left it at that and moved on to someone else; at other times he wouldn't take no for an answer and pushed and pushed until they either gave in or ran away. Because there was alcohol involved, it wasn't entirely clear to me whether these 'hook-ups' were consensual or whether the girls involved really knew what they were letting themselves in for. Either way, it was difficult to listen to these stories and not be worried about what had been happening between these teenagers. It appeared as though others in his peer group adopted the same tactic and attitude, although maybe not as prolifically as William.

What made the story so compelling was that William wasn't some poor, deprived, abused teenager. He went to a good school and, to all intents and purposes, had a happy family life.

Aside from the incidents themselves, which were shocking enough, it was clear that critical parts of William's life, namely his relational and sexual life, were being lived out in some alternative, perverse universe. Not only was there no monitoring of it, there was also no one to help him sort out what was appropriate and what, manifestly, was not.

'Have your parents ever talked to you about pornography, William?'

'No, they have never mentioned it. I think they are embarrassed about all that stuff.'

'So, what sort of stuff have you watched?'

William became uncomfortable in his chair.

'You know, stuff.'

'Yes, I know, but what sort of stuff?'

'It started out as sort of looking at women's boobs and stuff but all these other links come up. You just click and, well, I saw a lot of weird, violent stuff. I got curious. All my mates watch it and we talk about stuff we've seen and what sites show what. It's sort of normal, like talking about music or football. There is this weirdo at school, he watches a lot of "snuff movies", you know people being killed and stuff, that stuff is really, really sick.'

It was not difficult to see why William was having problems sleeping. William had a lot of trouble disentangling his more appropriate relational world view from his porn view and the work with him moved at a snail's pace.

Six months into our work William found himself being pursued by an adolescent girl who lived nearby. It was the perfect opportunity for us to talk about the way forward. William was in a complete muddle about his feelings for her. In his head this was all tied up with the images he'd been watching over the years. Adolescent love, holding hands, was something he hasn't ever thought about. His relations with the opposite sex in his mind were just about having sex in numerous different positions.

'The problem is, I really like her and I'm confused because I've only thought about sex as an act, a kind of performance, I hadn't thought about a relationship. Me and my mates just talk about the stuff we've seen and you know ...'

His sentence was left unfinished.

With a great deal of support William got through a few months without going further than holding hands and kissing. However, as intercourse became inevitable he worked himself up into a panic. He was anxious that it would turn into a performance of the kind he's watched so many times.

When he and his girlfriend did have sex, it was like many adolescent sexual encounters – pretty chaotic and largely unsatisfactory. However, for William it was a triumph of sorts: he didn't have any pornographic images intruding into his mind while he was with her. He was able to be with her without following the carefully scripted set-piece dramas that had become commonplace. It was a huge relief. He interpreted this as a sign that he was normal and not damaged by having watched such a lot of porn since he was 11.

Once William felt 'normal', he stopped coming to see me, which was a pity as I felt there was a lot more work to be done. All the same, the fact he did stop watching extreme porn and was in a real-life relationship was promising. All was not lost. Damage was well on the way to being undone.

A girl's perspective

I receive a call from Karen's mother in early June. She would like me to see her daughter. Something is wrong with Karen and has been since the Easter break. She has become withdrawn, irritable and her schoolwork has slipped. Her mother thinks an incident may have occurred on the school trip to France during the holidays but when she questions Karen, she is met with a flat denial.

Karen is 16. She sits curled up in the chair, her legs tucked under her bottom. She has long brown hair, which she hides behind. When I do catch a glimpse of her face the bags under her eyes give an impression that she hasn't slept for a week. She intermittently fiddles with the ends of her hair and bites her nails as she speaks. She rarely makes eye contact. It is obvious something is up but I'm not sure yet whether she will tell me. We talk about school and her life, but it is mostly small talk. We are not getting very far and I decide to take the bull by the horns and get to the heart of the matter.

'Karen, your mother thinks something happened when you went to France; she says you haven't been the same since. She seems to know you pretty well so, whatever happened, my guess is it must have had a big impact. Can you talk about it?'

Karen becomes agitated and anxious.

'You must promise not to tell anyone, I mean, really promise.'

'What we talk about is confidential.'

I can see that my response doesn't completely reassure her but her hesitation gives me a clue and a way in.

'Did something happen in France?'

'I'm not sure,' she replies.

'Can you say more?'

The story she recounts is both upsetting and extremely disturbing. The trip to France was great fun. There was a boy from the same year who she really liked and they spent quite a bit of time together. He apparently hassled her a bit sexually but she didn't think too much of it. I asked her what she meant by being hassled. She said he kept asking her if she would give him a blow job and other stuff. What took me by surprise was the casual way she seemed to shrug this off as part and parcel of the normal boy–girl dynamic.

It was the last night of the trip and they were all determined to have a celebration. Some of the boys managed to buy drink and smuggle it into the dorms where they were staying. She says she remembers they all got quite drunk. The boy asked her to go outside to have a cigarette, which was fine by her, but as soon as they got outside he started acting crazily. He started grabbing her and telling her all the stuff he would like to do with her (which, listening to her repeat it, it was obvious could have only come from watching porn). At this point she said she vaguely remembered starting to feel a little scared and she thinks she told him she wanted to go back inside. The next thing she remembers was being pushed to the ground outside the dorms and being made to have intercourse with him.

She sobs as she finishes telling the story.

'I feel so ashamed and disgusted. I just don't care about myself any more.'

'What makes you feel that, Karen? It sounds to me as though at the very least you've been the victim of a sexual assault.'

'That's what I think but I can't be sure. I asked him when we were back at school and he said I was drunk and agreed to it. I was drunk, I know that, but I can't remember whether I said yes or no. I think I asked him to stop but maybe I was too drunk to resist. I just don't have it clear in my mind.'

Karen was immensely relieved to have told someone. I was adamant that whether she was drunk or not she was still a victim and that she shouldn't feel it was her fault. This simple reassurance helped her to feel calmer. After much discussion she agreed that she would tell her parents. I was sure they had guessed that something like that had happened, although they might not have reckoned on the scale of it.

I saw Karen for several more sessions. It was enough to get her up and running. The talk with her parents had gone well – they had been attentive and supportive – and Karen decided she wanted to stop coming to the sessions. Coming to see me kept it alive, she explained. I think she just wanted to forget about it and get on with her life. I felt confident that her parents could help navigate future hurdles. Getting help earlier rather than later undoubtedly improved the chances of a good outcome for Karen.

There are many aspects of parenting that we would prefer not to deal with but this is definitely one where a head in the sand approach does not serve our teens well.

First, urgently, we need to ditch the denial defence, the one that goes along the lines of, 'My child would never do such a thing' or 'I have put a block on my computer so he can't watch it even if he wanted to.' It is true they may not watch it – or want to – but they sure as hell will hear about it and for boys and some girls of a certain age that will be on a daily basis. As parents, we vitally need to bring ourselves up to speed with the sorts of things they are watching, because what it is bears almost no relation to the tame, still photographs in *Playboy* that we might remember fondly from our own youths. I recently watched a supposedly serious discussion about the subject on TV. One member of the panel said she knew her son watched it upstairs in his bedroom but sighed indulgently that that was to be expected because, after all, 'boys will be boys'. The other churned out the hackneyed, 'In my day we only had magazines and they didn't do us any harm, hey ho,' to much laughter all round. It was resoundingly clear that none of them had watched any of the kind of pornography now freely available on the Internet to any child who can prod an iPad. If these uninformed spokespeople had actually bothered to look, however glancingly, they would without doubt have had a rather less gung-ho view.

Make a mental note of this next point:

> Watching pornography actively changes the adolescent brain and can have a hugely damaging effect on how they view all their subsequent relationships.

Watching porn immediately prompts a sharp spike in the amount of the chemical dopamine released into the brain. This is a neurotransmitter, which makes people feel focused and confident. But it also has consequences that are longer-term; it causes a desensitisation to the same erotic stimuli that turned the adolescent on in the first place. The user then craves more extreme porn to achieve the same feeling. Watching violent computer games has the same effect on their sensitivity to violence generally.

A study by the University of East London (September 2013) reported that a fifth of youths between the ages of 16 and 20 said they were 'dependent on porn as a stimulant for real sex'. Of those, 23 per cent said they had tried to stop watching it but could not and 13 per cent reported that the content they chose to view had become more and more extreme.

The ease of access to hard-core pornography operates against a background of confusing and potentially damaging changes in the sexual and relational dynamics between girls and boys. Romantic love used to be the starting point in the search for physical intimacy; nowadays the situation is reversed and physical intimacy is the starting point in the search for romantic love. Sexual exploration is and always has been part and parcel of adolescent life but, fuelled by pornography, what might have been a gentle exploration now looks more like a guided tour of hell. For many teenagers, porn is warping their view of what is sexually normal and acceptable. Most of the videos and the images have the same core relational dynamic in varying degrees, unless it's some specialised fetish site; namely male domination and female submission and humiliation – without, or more commonly with, violence. Parents of daughters cannot rest easy. Even if teenage girls don't want to watch porn, and they increasingly do, boys are coercing them into doing so.

There is statistical evidence available from the NSPCC which states that sexual violence within teenage relationships is increasing. This is directly related to the availability of hard-core pornography. William's story is the thin end of the wedge. If the boys are using pornography as their template, where does this leave the girls? In Karen's position perhaps? Objects to be used, debased and abused? My experience would suggest that girls are under tremendous pressure to 'perform'. Not to do so leaves them on the outside. As one older adolescent girl told me, 'I feel disgusted with myself for having done all that stuff when I was younger. What should have been an important and meaningful period in my life, turned into a nightmare, and the memory of it all still haunts me.'

So what are we to do about it? It is always more difficult to deal with parenting issues that we can't control. However vigilant and forceful we are we cannot prevent adolescents watching porn or engaging in porn-fuelled sexual exploration if that is what they want to do.

Firstly we need to register to our teen that we know what is out there. You, as a parent, are going to have to engage with the issue head-on. I recognise how difficult this is. Dealing with sexual matters with your children is awkward to say the least. When I have spoken about the matter to parents, I can see how uncomfortable they are with this area.

The reaction of your teenager to the question 'Have you seen or do you watch porn?' will give you a clear indication of where they are and what you need to do. Adolescents are curious and something forbidden is all the more enticing. So try and get a sense of whether curiosity is the driver or whether they are regular watchers, the difference matters.

In either case you need to outline the dangers: that it has nothing to do with real-life sexual relations and nothing to do with relationships. If your teenager is a regular watcher you need to get some sense of the amount of time they spend watching porn and the frequency. Is it every day, once a month, once a week? I'm not stupid enough to think you will get a truthful answer but it is possible to check the hard drive on their computer if you need to. This will undoubtedly ignite outrage and fury. Don't be put off, this is an important issue. Try not to go into a moral diatribe about porn's dangers. For most teenagers this tends to go in one ear and out the other. You need a more subtle approach. Ask them in a curious, rather than condemnatory, way if they have ever watched porn 'because you were talking to a friend who had caught her son doing so'. This opens the way to a potential dialogue.

For those parents who feel queasy about this topic, and it's perfectly understandable why this should be the case, I would suggest you do a little research. It is difficult to help your teenager if you don't have a real sense of what it is that they are watching.

Top Tips

- **Blocking the computer will not solve the problem.**
- **It is very difficult to start to help your adolescent with pornography if you don't have an idea of what it is they might be watching.**

- **Once you've done this and have seen what's out there, do not panic, hyperventilate and go at the problem with all guns blazing.**
  It is an educational and moral issue, so it needs to be talked about at the right time.
- **Keep focused on what he/she – and it usually is a he – made of it rather than turning it into an opportunity to blitz him with political correctness.**
  Engaging our teenage boys in an ongoing dialogue about pornography is as essential as teaching them to ride a bike. Above all, it is crucial that your teenage boy arrives at the understanding that pornography has nothing whatsoever to do with the development of a healthy relationship.
- **Despite this being a difficult and sensitive area, I can guarantee they will welcome your knowledge and help.**
  Pornography for this age group is more frightening than exciting.

Whatever you do, don't stick your head in the sand. Sex is a difficult topic. Make sure you talk about it with your teenager.

CHAPTER 8

Technology

Below is a family scenario that is so commonplace nowadays that we barely acknowledge it – it has become the new norm.

Mum and Dad and their three children are out for a Saturday lunchtime pizza. It has already been a little tense because 14-year-old Barney hadn't wanted to join them in the first place. He had been playing his new computer game – the latest war game – all morning. The graphics are the best yet, the body count grislier and higher than ever and, in Barney's words, it is 'awesome'. His parents hadn't been certain whether he should be playing such a game because it is, after all, an 18+, but he had persuaded them it was fine. He insisted all his friends had it, so why not him? Barney had at last reluctantly agreed to come to the restaurant. Sitting at the table, he has his headphones on and his smartphone in his pocket. His dad puts his BlackBerry down next to him and his mum does the same. His sister Emily, who is 12, walks to the table barely looking up from her phone and sits down without glancing up. Some of her friends are meeting up at a shopping centre and she desperately wants to know what is going on. Instagram is red hot with messages. The youngest, Billy, is seven. He has his iPad mini and is playing a game that he started in the car. This new gadget has been a godsend as far as his parents are concerned: it keeps Billy entertained – and, more importantly, quiet – for hours when the family are out and about. The only downside the parents have noted is that Billy seems to exhibit withdrawal symptoms when they take it away from him, and, as they can't face the fallout, they tend not to bother even to try any more.

A few moments after the family have taken their seats, the waiter comes over and leaves the menus on the table. Mum and Dad look at them and ask the kids what they want. No one responds, because they are all looking at the screens in front of them. Dad asks again, raising his voice slightly. Mum backs him up imploring the kids to concentrate. The children look up from their screens, barely glance at the menus, make a choice and go back to the screens. At that moment Dad's phone goes off. He excuses himself saying it's work. He stands up from the table and leaves the restaurant. Mum is left alone. She looks around wanting to talk to the children but all three of them are engaged elsewhere; she picks up her phone and checks her messages. She starts texting. Dad returns and apologises to no one in particular. In fact, the children hadn't even registered that he had left. The food arrives and the children are asked to put down their screens. As the meal starts, a conversation of sorts develops between the family members.

Barney is keen to extol the virtues of his latest video game and embarks on an excited explanation of who gets killed and how, in all its gory detail. Billy is enthralled by the explanation and wants to be allowed to play it. He wonders to himself if Barney will let him do so when Mum and Dad aren't looking. Dad's phone vibrates indicating a text or email. He picks it up and reads it. Barney sees his father has disengaged and his enthusiastic explanation grinds to a disappointing halt so he goes back to his screen. His father spots this and asks him to continue, but the moment has gone. Barney eats the remainder of his pizza in silence while glaring down at the screen right beside his plate. Mum and Dad make a few perfunctory efforts to start up a new conversation but none of the children seems interested. Emily can't wait for the meal to be over so she can get back home. One of her friends has agreed to call and tell her about all the excitements at the shopping centre. Billy is eating his pizza as fast as he can so he can get back to his game on the iPad. Actually, to waste no more time, he doesn't bother to finish his pizza at all.

This vignette from modern family life encapsulates the new world order: there is barely any connection or engagement between family members, let alone of any depth. Conversations and interactions are truncated and superficial. Quite simply, no one is interested in anyone else or, even less, wondering what they might be feeling or thinking. Their primary interest is in what is going on with their toys and in the disembodied worlds on which they are reporting.

This is a universal problem. As parents we are in uncharted territory. We are often either blinded by the excitement of the technology or at a complete loss as to know what to do about it. Does it matter? Yes, it does and I will explain why.

Here are a few facts that will give you a flavour of what this new world looks like for today's teenagers:

- Two-thirds of 12–15-year-olds in the UK now have a smartphone, according to a 2012 Ofcom report – a 50 per cent rise on the year before.
- Our UK teens spend on average nine hours a day digitally engaged.
- The average 13–17-year-old spends one hour and forty minutes a day on social media sites.
- They spend fifteen minutes a day taking selfies; one hour and twelve minutes a day playing computer games and one hour a day messaging friends (Logicalis Group, March 2016).

If you take out the number of hours they are disconnected from computers at school or sleeping, the statistics paint an interesting picture to say the very least.

What has interested and concerned me about this development is the nature of this closeness between teenagers and their 'toys' and the effect these have on their mind and on their relationships. Perhaps use of the word 'toys' doesn't really do justice to their sphere of influence because, of course, these 'toys' aren't 'toys' at all, in the old-fashioned sense of the word, meaning an object that engenders joy and playfulness and can give rise to imaginative and creative pleasure. These electronic gadgets are, in fact, more in the nature of life support systems because they are apparently as critical to these teenage lives as food and oxygen and water. They fiddle with them constantly. They put them down beside them only to cast longing glances at them moments later, glances that suggest that they see them as living entities necessitating care, attention and even affection. They stroke them, caress them and play with them. They are forever being distracted by the imagined needs and demands of these beloved electronic companions. God help family life if they lose them, resulting in the instant onset of paralysis and trauma!

What is it, though, that is so compelling about these quasi-animate friends? Why are they so vital? Like the real-life puppy or cuddly soft animal, they give succour and they endlessly entertain but, above all else, they are vital because they fill in disturbing gaps where boredom may lie, or frustration, or sadness, or low self-esteem, or fear. God forbid maybe even thoughts and ideas ... They distract these young people from the alarming business of facing the world and confronting themselves.

The Impact of Technology on Relationships

It is clear that these 'things' have and are changing the way children relate to themselves, to others and to the world around them. It is becoming harder to access what is going on in their minds. Their primary preoccupation and main activity are 'distractions' – and so it is that they lose touch with any sense of what is really going on inside their own heads. And if they are unable to properly access what is going on inside their own heads then it surely follows that they won't have much idea or curiosity about what might be going on inside the heads of others. It might be argued that some features of these devices, with their instant access on a whole new scale, promote an untold connection to others the globe over. But it is the nature of the connectedness that is important. Meaningful, person-to-person connectedness is not the same as cyber-connectedness. Cyber-connectedness is random at worst (talking/communicating to strangers) and limited at best (it is necessarily one-dimensional). True connection between people involves the processing of a whole range of complex non-verbal communications; facial recognition, subtleties of tone, hand movements, and so forth. All these factors combine to contribute to an accurate reading of others' intentions and their states of mind. Understanding and interpreting all this, even on an unconscious level, takes time to practise and learn, first in the home and later in the wider world, among peers and strangers. It is part of what it is to be a human being. Cyber-connection is just words, all words and nothing else, and therefore is entirely one-dimensional. If real-life connectedness is compromised and reduced in favour of cyber-'connectedness', which isn't really connectedness at all, then our children are necessarily going to be severely handicapped in their adult relationships, of every kind.

I firmly believe that we are witnessing an erosion of our adolescents' capacity to 'meaningfully' engage with themselves and other people. Put simply, their capacity to develop and sustain relationships that are not merely superficial is under attack.

We are rightly concerned about the safety of our teenagers and want to know who they are with and where they are. But we are on less solid ground when it comes to where on earth they reside in cyberspace – and they could be *anywhere*, not just a choice of one or two friends' houses, two pubs and a club in the city centre. If we are honest we probably don't know how much time they spend looking at a screen or have much idea what effect, if any, screen life is having on their developing minds.

It is only belatedly that we are waking up to the impact that this technology can have. We see on the news or read in the headlines the horror stories of adolescent online bullying and suicide. But it is not these more extreme tragedies, still thankfully relatively rare, on which I wish to focus. Instead, my immediate concern is the more long-term and less obvious effect this technology has on young people's ability to develop sustaining and nurturing relationships. It is commonplace, and may seem more prosaic in comparison to death and destruction, but it is still tragic after its own fashion. Slowly but surely the addiction to technology is eroding the capacity to develop and sustain the kind of relationships that we know promote psychological and emotional well-being.

What might the future look like?

Addiction to the moment and the stimulation it provides is giving rise to attention spans that are worryingly short. This is not a dystopian vision. It is now a fact of life. A future adolescent's world might look something like this:

- Someone whose primary relationships are with their 'toys', addicted to the moment and the stimulation they provide.
- Someone with a short attention span.
- Someone with very little sense of either themselves or others.
- Someone connected to the whole world but disconnected from those around them.

Fantastical maybe, but ...

There is as yet no definitive research on how all this new technology is affecting teenagers, but one would have to be blind or in serious denial to suppose it is only a force for good. While many researchers wax lyrical about the new generation of teenagers who can flip between tasks with ease, others darkly warn of the dangers of 'digital dementia'. We don't know exactly how all this hyperstimulation will shape the adolescent brain, but we know that it does, and will continue to, affect it. It is suggested by some researchers that while teenagers will get better at multitasking, this will come at a price. Their attention span will be diminished and their capacity to reflect on things in depth will be compromised.

W hatever our view of this new world, it is self-evident that time spent in digital engagement comes at the cost of time spent face-to-face with real people including with the self.

Developing meaningful connectedness

It is critical for the healthy psychological development of our children that they are gradually able to move away from a world of instant gratification – a world which is more associated with the baby or young child – to the grown-up world of delayed gratification, or, indeed, the absence of any gratification at all. The space between thinking about and yearning for something and actually obtaining it is when we think, reflect and create. There is research that suggests that the capacity to delay gratification is a significant factor in living a successful life. Any parent will tell you this is a painful, difficult and arduous journey. The problem is our 'electronic' friends corrupt this process and work in the opposite direction. They are the finest purveyors of instant gratification on the planet. They push us back to an infantile world where what we want is readily, constantly and immediately available. A flick of a switch will take you anywhere you want to go. Frustrated, worried, bored, time to kill? Don't worry, help is at hand – gratification is at your very fingertips.

In order for our teens to manage their own thoughts and feelings, and later the thoughts and feelings of others, they need time and absence from stimulation and distractions. In this space they can begin to reflect consciously or unconsciously on the question of what is happening or has happened, what they feel and why. The adolescent has much psychological and emotional work to do. The boredom, the listlessness, the mooching, the chilling, the procrastinating, the lounging, the irritability so evident among teenagers, are all the outward signs of internal work being done, albeit rather painfully. Making sense of himself and the world around him is crucial. And if it is successful, it can be translated into making sense of others and others' worlds. These are the foundations of meaningful connectedness.

Some might argue that electronic toys offer more opportunity for connection with others than ever before, and not less. There is, certainly, some truth to this argument, at least in theory. Thanks to new technology, you can now FaceTime Granny in New Zealand from the shopping centre on a Saturday afternoon, but this is not its only purpose and not the only one employed by its users. Besides the obvious benefits, a whole host of less edifying pastimes are on offer. Games and reading tweets about what type of sandwich a complete stranger chose for her lunch kills time between activities or events ('kills' being the operative word). These cyber activities distract teenagers from what is going on inside them and are being used as a vehicle for evacuating the raw emotional data that, when it has the space to be developed and refined, produces and cultivates ideas. A dispute or misunderstanding between friends is now an opportunity for the creation of a mini TV drama, the object of which is to create a momentary excitement which fills the gap between an otherwise listless, uncertain present and the next big event. It is also a way of seeing off the accompanying psychological discomfort. The opportunity to ponder upon the misunderstanding to seek to understand it, and perhaps learn from it, is lost.

Some may ask what is wrong with that, with not privately processing more negative day-to-day experiences but instead either creating a merry drama out of them for all and sundry or simply passing them by unreconstructed. My answer to this is that containing anxiety and distress, processing feelings and events, alone or face-to-face with supportive family and friends, are the building blocks of healthy psychological development.

It is futile to imagine that we can somehow stop this new and constantly evolving world impacting on our teenagers' lives, but what we can do is engage with it in a thoughtful and constructive way so that we can retain the best aspects, and mediate the worst. It also really requires us to think about it as a family. There are two strands to this that we can usefully concentrate on:

1. The content (what they look at or listen to): this is difficult to manage, but not impossible.
2. The amount of time spent engaged with it: this is perfectly possible to control, but it needs a plan and a certain amount of resilience on our part.

Let's look at the various forms this technology takes and put in place some practical strategies to help your teen manage their addiction to distractions.

Social Networking

Facebook, Twitter, Snapchat, Instagram, Tumblr, Twitter, LinkedIn ... these social networking sites and many more besides are all readily available to our children. One tap of the button connects them to the world. How marvellous that so many people can be contacted so widely, quickly and efficiently. How rather less marvellous that the technology is not neutral. In December 2016 the NSPCC delivered a report stating that 18.778 children aged 11–18 were admitted to hospital for self-harm, with the most at-risk group being the 14–17 age group. The report went further and suggested that the major cause was exposure to social media. Peter Wanless, chief executive of the NSPCC, said that teenagers felt a constant need to keep up with friends on their smartphones and were never able to switch off. Nicole's story that follows is less serious but nevertheless illustrative of the dilemmas teenagers now face.

Fourteen-year-old Nicole's parents have become really concerned about her. Nicole was, up until a few months ago, a bright, vivacious young teenager. In recent months she has become anxious, argumentative and prone to breaking down crying. They are sure something untoward is going on but Nicole won't tell them what it is. She has agreed, however, to come and see me.

Nicole takes a long while to settle in the room. She is small and rather immature for her age. She is more of a 14- going on 13-year-old. She is agitated and fidgets incessantly. If I didn't know better I might think she had some kind of attention deficit disorder. She tries to start talking but stops seemingly on the verge of tears. When she does get going it's an unstoppable outpouring of confusions, anxieties and upsets, interspersed with tears. She has discovered the teenage world of friends and social networking. She texts, posts and speaks to friends at every available moment. Everything in the day, however trivial, is commented upon and dissected, often in minute detail. It starts in the morning on the way to school and continues until she goes to sleep at night. The blur of excitement she feels about this new world is matched by her realisation that it is far from benign. The inane but essentially harmless communications are punctuated by bouts of teasing and sexual comments. One girl is teasing her because she has small breasts, while another thinks she's fat (she isn't). Some of the girls had a sleepover, which she didn't know about and wasn't invited to. She asked one of the girls why and was told she was boring. Her mind is in turmoil and completely consumed by it all.

Her outpourings are punctuated by: 'What should I say?', 'What did she mean?', 'Should I respond or leave it?', 'But if I say this and she says that then what will X think?'

Round and round she goes barely drawing breath. I make what I hope is a calming comment but she is unable to take it in. She is desperately trying to get control of a world that seems to her to be spinning out of control. As we speak her phone pings constantly as the messages come flying in.

I ask her if she minds turning it off.

'I can't, I am waiting for one of my friends to message me about the sleepover.'

It feels as though Nicole's friends have invaded my consulting room, essentially a private space for therapist and teenager. This must be how she feels. I insist she turns her phone off and reluctantly she does. The change in her mood is palpable. Nicole visibly relaxes.

I ask whether she ever turns her phone off. She says she does before she goes to sleep at night but has it on silent at school. She says that she is not supposed to but everyone does and the school never checks. I ask her why she hasn't been able to talk to her parents about these issues. She says she is afraid that they will take her phone away.

After much hesitation and cajoling Nicole agrees to have a joint meeting with her parents and try to broker a deal about it. Her parents are sensitive and thoughtful, they just hadn't quite got up to speed with Nicole's rapidly expanding social world and had no idea she was under so much pressure. We agree that Nicole needs respite from this social world rather than being banned from it. They set a cut-off time in the evening when Nicole is 'offline' (phone and computer). Nicole looks crestfallen at the idea and mounts a staunch defence for 24/7 usage. She argues vehemently that she will miss out and therefore be left out. Her parents reassure her that they are not suggesting a block ban but respite. They haggle over the exact timing of the respite but eventually come to an agreement.

Nicole's mother calls a week later and tells me that Nicole is much more settled. They still have the occasional argument about when to switch off the devices but, by and large, the 'respite' is working.

This unremarkable story contains a critical dilemma for modern family life. How much 'intrusion' into family life should we allow? To my mind it's helpful to think about the importance of adolescents needing respite from the incessant demands of his or her peers; a time to process the day; a time to think his or her own thoughts, free from the barrage of other adolescents' baggage; a time to reconnect with family. It's my view that there should be a cut-off time in the evening when phones should be handed in to parents: between 7 and 8pm is late enough.

In her book *Mind Change*, the eminent neuroscientist Susan Greenfield points out some worrying side effects of social networking. She cites one of the most important from a study which shows that Facebook users are more satisfied with their life when their 'friends' are regarded as their very own personal 'audience', an 'audience' to whom they respond unilaterally. Multiple communications with this online group are rated more satisfying than mere one-to-one exchanges. As Greenfield points out, this opens up the rather bizarre possibility that the excitement of reporting and receiving information becomes more rewarding than the actual experience.

Greenfield also presents evidence that suggests teenagers think little of giving out personal details of their lives to someone they don't know from Adam, including photographs and physical descriptions.

Another of her significant findings is that, because of the anonymity provided by sites, users tend to exaggerate aspects of their personality and so it is that the presentation of the self may bear little relation to the person in real life.

What Greenfield's insights reveal is that the use of sites and the interaction of their users are more complex than they might at first seem. The concept of audiences, of the giving up of personal – sometimes intimate – information to strangers, of the creation of other selves, is all just part and parcel of social networking. There is now an absence of the kind of psychological constraints which we have forever taken for granted and which have always been automatically provided by the mediating presence of face-to-face communication and non-verbal cues. This has led to the development of a distorted version of the user and a warped version of interaction. For teenagers who are in the delicate process of trying to discover who they really are, this territory is fraught indeed because the online self does not correspond to the true one. Greenfield notes that this online self might be thought of as a 'hoped-for self', a sort of idealised one. The danger is the developing gap between the two selves, especially for those teenagers with low self-esteem. It would not be difficult to imagine such a teenager identifying himself with the 'hoped-for' self at the complete expense of the real self, a psychological distortion ripe for a very insecure sense of identity and with potentially disastrous consequences. (It's worth holding in mind that 75 per cent of adult mental health issues start before the age of 18 and that many of these issues are a result of not feeling secure or having any real sense of self.)

Greenfield stresses it is not absolutely clear what effect all this cyber-communication will have, but it is possible that what might be lost for good is the capacity for people to read others' intentions and thoughts accurately.

To my mind, there is scope enough for misinterpretation and misunderstanding in the real world as it is, and that is with all the tools at our disposal of critical non-verbal communications and face-to-face encounters. Without them, teenagers will grow up completely incapable of being able properly to understand their fellow human beings and absolutely unable to begin to interpret what might be going on in the mind of another person. The whole notion of empathy stands to be blown into the ether.

Mobile Phones

The fact that so much of social media is accessed by mobile phone raises a number of important questions about how and when we allow our teenagers to use them. Giving children mobile phones seems to be one of those unquestioned rites of passage: 'I want one, I get one', no questions asked. I am never quite sure what the rationale is behind giving one to a preadolescent child other than as an expensive toy. Do they use it to arrange play dates? Do they need it to be in contact with their friends and classmates? Are they out and about enough to warrant parents keeping careful tabs on their whereabouts? I suspect the answer to those questions is no. If they are going out with friends or to an activity is it not better to give them a phone while they are out and take it back when they return? If we are honest, most parents cave in under the weight of the 'everyone has one' argument. The thought of their children being social pariahs if they don't have the latest phone is a step too far.

I realise that most parents reading this will have already made choices about this. In fact, the statistics suggest that I'm swimming against the tide here: a survey by the health insurers Aviva in January 2017 stated that 80 per cent of children have a mobile by the age of 12. So, by the time your child gets to adolescence, they have probably already had a phone for two or three, or even four, years.

The next question that needs consideration is exactly what sort of phone your adolescent should have and that requires us to think about what they need a phone for. Most parents would argue its main purpose is to be able to contact friends and family and to keep tabs on where they are should anything untoward happen. If this is the case, they do not need more than a basic phone.

However, more often than not we end up providing them with an all-singing, all-dancing smartphone, effectively a full-on entertainment centre that can be accessed 24/7. Maybe they can watch a film or TV show during their lunch break, perhaps a few YouTube clips, listen to some music or watch a bit of porn on the school bus ... or even send a naked picture of themselves to their prospective girlfriend or boyfriend. It seems to me that we are inviting trouble. If you are really serious about getting to grips with these issues I would give a great deal of thought about whether your teen needs a smartphone or not. There is no doubt that a decision not to give them a smartphone is likely to cause a storm in many cases. But 'storm levels' shouldn't enter the equation when making parenting decisions.

With phones comes, of course, security, and questions such as 'Should they be allowed a password?' arise. The unequivocal answer to this question is no. There are some very sound reasons why this should be the case. You are unlikely to let your teenager go out without knowing where they are going and, in the same way, you need to keep tabs on what they are doing on their phone (and their computer for that matter). You might reconsider this when they are 16 but not before. This doesn't mean you will be checking their phone every five minutes, but from time to time you might need to know who they are messaging and what the content of those messages is. If they have a smartphone you need to know what they are looking at. Many of you will have read about teenage 'sexting' plus or minus explicit photos. These can be both damaging and upsetting when shared with other teenagers. Of course you can speak to your teenager about the dangers of this, but for many teenagers it is all the more exciting if it's forbidden, and since when did adolescents always listen to their parents? Getting access to their phones is part of being able to keep abreast of what's happening.

But the really persuasive argument for not allowing them passwords is for you to be able to monitor what comes in. Online grooming is very common. Adults posing as young teenagers befriending your son or daughter are sadly part of today's world. Remember that however smart and switched on you believe your adolescent to be, they are still vulnerable.

Most parents I speak to 'sort of' agree with this view but find the 'invasion of my privacy' argument allied to a ranting teenager too much to deal with. Do not under any circumstances allow a password for an under-16. This is an issue of online safety, not a control issue.

Now that your teen has a phone when should they turn it off? Many of the adolescents I see have their phones on all night and bedtime is a prime time for texting and chatting. There are good scientific and psychological reasons for having a cut-off time. Scientists are cautioning against using light-emitting devices before bed. These devices emit what is called 'blue light' and blue light mimics the effects of the sun and tricks the body into thinking it should be awake. It stops the production of the hormone melatonin that makes us feel sleepy.

An unpleasant or misunderstood text message is enough to disturb a teenager's night's sleep. I am in favour of a cut-off time – between 7 and 8pm – when they hand their phone in until the next morning. There are two compelling reasons for this:

1. They need respite from the interminable chatter of teenage life.
2. They need to reconnect with family life.

Unfortunately there is a sting in the tail here: they can't reconnect with family life if you as parents are on your phones all evening. Why not consider a family shut-down? If you do need to have your phone on for work in the evening, is it not possible to deal with it after the children have gone to bed? I recognise this isn't straightforward, but you can't be fully there for your adolescent if you are on your phone all the time.

Top Tips

- **Does your adolescent really need a smartphone?**
- **Broker 'respite' time.**
  If it can't be brokered and adhered to, impose it.
- **Do not allow mobile phones or any electronics in their bedroom at night.**
  Bedtime is a prime texting time for adolescents and mobile phones or other electronic devices can severely disrupt sleep.

- **Do not allow social networking sites, such as Facebook, phones or computers to have passwords or codes that block you.**
  The argument that your adolescent needs their privacy has no validity whatsoever. The younger adolescent is vulnerable and it is your job to protect them.

If adolescents are spending too much of their non-school life umbilically attached to computer games, pornography, social media and all the other accoutrements of adolescent life, then we as parents are putting their capacity to develop relationships at serious risk.

CHAPTER 9

Gaming

Ethan is 17 and, as far as I can gather, for the last two years has spent most of his non-school time in his bedroom playing computer games, but his habit in fact goes way back. His parents have by and large left him to it, having not quite known what to do but always clinging on to the hope that he would 'grow out of it' sooner rather than later. He seems to have had a normal childhood but, at the age of 14, he decided to give up playing football for the school team and dropped most of his friends. He gradually withdrew from the real world. He is fairly good academically and gained some decent GCSEs. It's not clear why he suddenly stopped developing. In my experience in the absence of an 'identifiable trauma', like the death of a parent, finding a cause can often be a fruitless search. One adolescent's hiccup is another's insurmountable challenge. Things have come to a head because Ethan has been asked to think about university and he is adamant that he does not want to go. His parents have accepted this, albeit through gritted teeth. The difficulty from their point of view is that Ethan does not want to entertain any other options either. Communication has broken down at home. Ethan refuses to speak to them and only comes out of his bedroom for food and to go to school.

Before I go any further I will come clean over a deal his parents and I made with Ethan over the computer games. The more astute readers might be wondering how I managed to get this reluctant young man to come to therapy at all let alone on a regular basis. The simple answer is that we made a pact whereby in exchange for coming to our sessions, he was allowed to play at the weekend. Yes, I broke one of my golden rules – I did a deal – but to my mind it was that or nothing. The fact that Ethan came in at all was nothing short of a miracle as far as I was concerned and offered a glimmer of hope for the future.

Reluctant is a description that would not do sufficient justice to his manner when we first met; intransigent, hostile and uncommunicative are nearer the mark. He wore a hoodie pulled up over his head, huge headphones protruded from beneath it and a scarf covered most of his face. He looked as though he was about to take an Arctic hike as opposed to have a consultation in the West End of London in mid-May. Rather bizarrely he was also wearing gloves.

I opened with a tentative question about the 'threat' (part of the deal to get him to see me) which was to disconnect him from the Internet and games.

'Yeah, well they [his parents] can try but I'll leave home or kill myself.'

I took this with a pinch of salt and in my head translated it to mean he was passionately attached to his gaming.

'That's quite a statement,' I told him. 'You'd actually consider dying for it?'

'It is my life,' he countered emphatically, and then proceeded to tell me about his online existence, all the 'friends' [my emphasis] he had met from all over the world through playing games, including his Russian girlfriend who lives somewhere in Siberia.

'What do you talk to them about?' I asked.

'The games.'

'Anything else?'

For the first time I glimpsed some hesitation. It was as if he had to stop himself from saying something like, 'Well, what else is there?' He knew where I was going with this – he's not completely out of it.

'No, but they are proper friends.'

'Well, I am sure they are, but they're not ones you're likely ever to meet are they? Do you think it's easier to deal with friends when they are so far away or even unknown? You can sort of control your relational life with the click of a button. You don't have to deal with them face-to-face really.'

I could see I'd pushed him quite hard and he didn't like it, but he didn't flounce out so I knew I'd still got some engagement with him and so pressed on.

'Maybe it's a kind of fantasy life, Ethan. You know, one that remains in your head and is safe because it never gets tested. You say you've got a girlfriend in Russia but you've never met her and are unlikely to, she's a sort of virtual girlfriend isn't she? Maybe it's easier to have a virtual girlfriend than have to deal with a real one.'

It was clear from his face that the hostility had gone. He looked deflated and crestfallen. His carefully constructed alternative world was gossamer thin and it had just been punctured.

Over the following few months Ethan returned to see me often. The sessions were painful and hard work. I realised that his gaming was the least of his problems. Ethan was a 13-year-old in a 17-year-old's body. He hadn't done any of the work adolescents need to do – the wondering, the curiosity about life just isn't there – and he had never been given the space to flourish. His conversation was superficial, juvenile and banal. Occasionally the internal light bulb flickered into life and we seemed to be getting somewhere but it quickly dimmed. He struggled to do any real thinking. He looked bewildered when I asked him what he could draw from a story he had just recounted. If I didn't know better, I would think he had some mild learning difficulty. His addiction to distractions (in this case his gaming) had left him with not a single real meaningful relationship to speak of. He would have to start all over again and, at 17, that was a tall order. Worryingly, he had not the first clue as to the urgency of the need to get down to it or the remotest notion of how to start.

Ethan's story is an interesting one but his saving grace is that he managed to reach the age of 14 relatively intact. In other words, while he had quite a hearty relationship with the technological world before then, it wasn't all-consuming. Total immersion only occurred post-14.

What I had to do in the sessions was less about unpacking and analysing what was in his mind, and more about getting him to start thinking, start reflecting.

At first Ethan struggled like a child learning to swim. Our frequent detours into the world of girls and sex at least guaranteed his attention and a certain sense of anticipation. Over the months I became aware that the light bulb was beginning to stay on for longer than at first, and it was possible to see a reawakening of the 14-year-old who had gone missing for three years. As often with male adolescents, it was the arrival of a girl into his life that provided the turbo charge for growth. Ethan, though not particularly engaging or interesting away from the subject of computer games, was in fact a very good-looking young man. An intelligent and lovely young woman swept him up once he started to look vaguely engaged with the world around him. Surprise, surprise, she captured his attention in ways I could not. She detested his computer gaming and, after numerous rows, managed to get him to stop. She dragged him around like a new puppy to various social events. Slowly but surely he reacquainted himself with the real world and, much to his surprise, began to enjoy it.

When he stopped coming to see me in the May before his A levels, it was obvious to everyone that Ethan was a very different young man. From time to time he could still give an excellent impression of someone who had undergone a frontal lobotomy, but at least he was in the world. I had a note from his parents telling me that he had done well in his A levels and had decided to apply for university the following year. One hopes that the real world and those in it will engage him enough to stop him retreating into the erstwhile, empty but dangerous world of games and endless distractions. What is certain is that had he been allowed to remain away from reality, in the realms of dubious cyber-space, his actual life might well have been a mess.

For adults of a certain generation gaming is foreign, unexplored territory whereas for today's teenagers – boys especially – it is their lifeblood. The gap between the two is where matters become messy and confusing.

Here are some statistics from a Public Health England report (28 August 2013):

- Excessive screen time – more than four hours a day – is linked to increased anxiety and depression.
- The amount of time children are playing online games is going up all the time and is driven by the availability and ubiquity of computer games.
- Between 2006 and 2010, the proportion of children playing computer games for more than two hours a night increased from 14 per cent to 20 per cent in girls, and 42 per cent to 55 per cent in boys.

Imperial College London runs Britain's only Internet addic-tion centre and the majority of Internet addicts are gamers. These young people have stopped attending school or university and are unable to connect with anything outside the game in hand. There is some evidence that prolonged use of the Internet (especially games) can reveal abnormalities in the brains of adolescents. But like so much of modern technology we just don't know for sure what the longer term effects will be.

I realise that gaming is part of modern life. My point is it is not a neutral activity. It is fun but it can also be damaging. As a parent, you need to have a plan. Do you allow your teenager to play at the weekends only or do you allow them to play every day, or a variation of the two? There are two aspects to bear in mind when devising some ground rules for your teen: games are programmed to keep you playing for longer and longer, and every hour spent playing a computer game is one less hour spent engaged with the world.

Let's start by debunking the myth that age-appropriate certificates protect our adolescents ... they don't. Getting round them is meat and drink to adolescents. Here is a familiar scam: go to a store, stand outside and pay someone a few pounds to buy the game for you. Put it in a 12+ case at home and no one knows.

Most teenagers play games on their computer or Xbox, some for longer than others, but increasingly games are being even more easily accessed via smartphones. As a parent you need to make an assessment of both the amount of time your teen plays for and how easily they can stop. This is critical as there are clear dangers from gaming for long periods of time. It is also important to identify which type of game your child is playing online. There are essentially two types: first-person shooter games and multiple-player role-playing games. The first involves a good deal of fighting and killing. The second does too, as well as the creation of an avatar (or gamer-controlled character or alter ego). For the first-person shooters there are obvious disadvantages inherent in the amount of aggression and violence being processed by the player. For players of multi-player role-playing games, there is the added risk that the child can all too readily develop an overly strong attachment to the avatar to the detriment of his real self.

The valid point made by those who see nothing wrong with gaming is that part of the essence of gaming is that it is consequence-free. In other words, actions do not have consequences. But this is no free pass as it is manifestly at odds with the aim of adolescent parenting which is that precisely the opposite is the case in real life. There are also concerns that this 'world without consequences' which teenagers so readily inhabit, might encourage behaviour in real life that is even more reckless and risky than it is already.

Despite all this, the critical question here is whether your child can control his gaming. By this I mean is he able to turn it off after an agreed time period and does he suffer from what might be loosely called withdrawal symptoms (usually a temper tantrum or extreme agitation)? If he can stop (and it is usually a he), fine; if he can't, then there is definitely a problem and you have to intervene. You must broker a deal with your gamer. This is a very clear and non-negotiable agreement about when to play and for how long. I am in favour of week-ends only. The excitement generated by the thought of being allowed to play during the week not only interferes with family life but it also may compromise attitudes to homework and other activities. Some downtime playing games at the weekend – an hour or two maximum – is fine. If your teen can't stick to it, that is, adhere to the rules regarding when he plays, or has an adverse reaction to having to stop, then you have to consider a total ban. It is draconian, I know, but are you going to spend hours of family time, every time, having arguments about how long they can play for? The question, now, is not about gaming but all about your relationship with your teenager. Are you as parents avoiding doing something because you are frightened of the repercussions or impact it will have on the family as a whole? If the answer to that question is yes, then you are opting out of your responsibilities and your teen's problems are only just beginning.

Another thing to consider is this: gaming provides the perfect retreat from the developmental process. If an adolescent lacks confidence or feels insecure, why would they do anything other than spend all day and most of the night playing computer games? These provide a lovely, comforting parallel universe where they feel all-powerful and totally in control. This is the whole point, of course, and you can acknowledge the attraction. But it is nothing to do with the bodily world, which they actually inhabit, out of which they are opting so manifestly, but with which they must urgently engage if they are going to avoid potentially serious problems. I have seen many adolescents over recent years, like Ethan described above, whose sole preoccupation has been gaming. Their capacity to relate outside of this narrow corridor is severely impaired and as a consequence predictably creates huge problems for face-to-face interactions and their interaction with the world around them.

The jury is still out on how damaging gaming is but, again, neuroscientist Susan Greenfield makes an obvious point: whatever it is that we practise repeatedly will affect the brain and so it stands to reason that if we practise aggression, we will begin to think and react more aggressively and will become better at being aggressive.

Tragic and dramatic stories about the dangers of the Internet and new technologies emerge on a weekly basis. Harrowing though they are for the families involved, they focus our attention on only one area, and that is content. We falsely believe that if we can control the less salubrious and more dangerous games and sites, then our teenager will be just fine. Hell, no. I have seen parents who have told me that their adolescent is 'okay' because he only plays age-appropriate computer games and he doesn't use social media or the Internet, much. When I ask them how long he plays for they will often say every day, for hours – and hours – only ever emerging from his room to use the bathroom, collect a sandwich from the kitchen or grunt menacingly at anyone who fleshly wanders into view. Content may be seen as the car crash, but the amount of hours nosed to the screen is what we should really be worried about.

What to Do

The main issue here is that many parents have not given the matter of gaming sufficient thought, and that is because they don't really know what they are dealing with. We don't let our children eat sweets all day and night because we know sugar plays havoc with their teeth, their behaviour and their metabolisms. We don't fully understand, though, what impact the relatively new all-singing, all-dancing cyber distractions will have on them in the longer term. We are ourselves too often in the thrall of the latest technology to give it much thought and, if we are honest, we find it a relief that the new gadgets and games keep the children quiet and stop them from pestering us so we can get on with our own lives. They act as a kind of legitimate parenting valium, but by the time we are up to speed with what the implications might be for our children, the horse will have bolted, so to speak.

Adolescents need boundaries and constraints and most parents provide them some of the time. Even so, the Internet with its many features – social networking, games, pornography and the rest – provides a veritable 24/7 funfest any place, anywhere, and at the touch of a button. It is a parallel universe that does not know the meaning of the word boundaries. How on earth do we begin to control and contain it?

Wonderful though the new technology is, it is not the same as playing Monopoly – gaming has some serious downsides that you need to think about. You need to consider what place it has in your home and what kind of exposure you feel is appropriate. I have detailed that I am in favour of weekend playing, and then for a maximum of two hours only, no extras. This sort of structure is clear and minimises the aggravation and interference in family life. Many reading this might already have teens who play games a lot more than I have advocated. But I don't think you have to worry about what has gone before – you are perfectly at liberty to change the system as you see fit. Again, don't be put off by the threat of adolescent melt-down. It is your prerogative and responsibility to make the rules; family life shouldn't be a democracy. If your son wants to play computer games do the deal and stick to it. Whatever you do, don't waste time negotiating a new deal every day or every week. Remember, no deal, no game. Two hours at the weekend is a maximum.

Top Tips

- **Is your adolescent telling you the truth about the amount of time they are playing?**
- **Are they withdrawing from family and friends and becoming isolated?**

- Have you noticed that they seem more anxious and restless when not gaming?
- Have you noticed that they seem to be thinking obsessively about gaming even while doing other things?
- Under no circumstances allow them to play games alone in their bedroom for any significant length of time (more than an hour).
- Have you been able to broker a proper deal around when they can and can't play?
- Are you avoiding taking action because you can't stand the aggravation that it will necessarily entail?

You must have a family rule about the use of technology in the home. Once you have made clear what it is, stick to it.

CHAPTER 10

Education

'I tried not to let school interfere with my education.'
Mark Twain

Janine is 15 and starting the second year of her GCSE course. She attends the local comprehensive and is an able enough young girl who should do well in her exams. Janine's parents didn't go to university and they are keen that she goes. They feel it will give her opportunities they didn't have. All it requires at this moment is for Janine to put in her best effort and all will be well, but right now she is doing the opposite and seems to be losing focus.

Her parents are concerned that if she carries on like this she won't gain good enough grades. They describe her as a 'lovely' girl but one who has always been lazy. They have tried talking to her but she says everything is fine and they should just leave her alone.

When I meet Janine I find a humorous, sociable and quick-witted young teenager. She is full of energy; the great passion in her life is music. I don't see or hear anything that concerns me. She's not a problem at school. On the contrary, she is well liked by the staff and her friends.

According to her parents, though, she is going out with her friends too much and she leaves assignments until the last minute and then panics about getting them done in time. She has also been talking a lot about leaving school as she doesn't really want to stay on and do her A levels. Her parents feel this is a terrible waste and they can't get to grips with what she is doing.

Janine is having a crisis of sorts, a loss of nerve. This kind of crisis is typical and perfectly normal for her age group. She is having doubts about herself and is anxious that she won't make it through her GCSE's. She knows what she has to do but she can't seem to knuckle down. Her anxiety about the outcome is stopping her from working properly. The exams are a kind of rite of passage and she is using typical magical teenage thinking: if I ignore it it won't happen.

Janine's parents are at a loss as to know what they could do to alter the situation.

In my experience, what doesn't work in situations like this is the guilt trip – 'Don't you realise you're messing up your future?' – a trap into which so many exasperated parents readily fall. All this line of enquiry does is create further anxiety and make the situation worse. What teenagers need instead is something practical, a non-negotiable structure around them, not as a punishment but to contain their anxiety. And by non-negotiable, I mean non-negotiable. Something along the lines that they absolutely cannot go out at the weekend unless they put their best effort into their school work. Then set up a timetable for their work each day after school and monitor it. You have money, their mobile phone and perhaps the Internet as your bargaining tools. Present it as a fait accompli and don't engage with any of the outrage that will most certainly greet your presentation.

Some of you reading this might be thinking that my suggestions seem straightforward and a touch simplistic, but the impact is all in the implementation. If it is wishy-washy, you are scuppered. Of course, your teen isn't going to jump for joy at your structure, quite the opposite. They will kick up a huge fuss, the scale of which will depend on how frightened they feel. Your job is to stand firm in the line of fire and guide them through. Whatever you do, do not negotiate, do not buckle.

This is how it looks. Write down a list of your teen's work and study expectations. That way there is no room for confusion. Make time at the end of the week to review their performance and if they tick all the boxes the weekend is theirs, but if they miss just one then they forgo their weekend. Don't discuss or explain. The deal is simple.

Janine's parents quickly took all this advice on board. Much to their surprise, Janine hardly batted an eyelid. On the contrary, she seemed almost relieved. She got good grades in her GCSEs and stayed on for her A levels. With this rite of passage under her belt she should be set fair for her A levels.

Janine's story is an important one. All adolescents have anxieties about self-worth and doubts about their abilities. There is nothing to be gained by going on about the importance of the challenges ahead or berating them for their 'avoidance' tactics. What your teen needs is a watertight strategy that contains them and outlines a way forward, a strategy with no wriggle room. This has the effect of quieting the anxieties and giving them real focus. As a postscript I don't buy into the idea of 'laziness'. The issue that underlies this is instead fear of failure.

What is 'Education'?

The issue of a child's education is guaranteed to catapult most parents' anxiety through the roof. It is a minefield of confusions, misunderstandings and prejudice. Parents spend fortunes on it; they move house in the hope of getting it; they even discover religion in pursuit of it. This anxiety increases as their sons and daughters move through adolescence because the reality check, in the form of exams, looms large on the horizon.

Quite what this 'good education' consists of is unclear. In my experience parents know a lot about a school's examination results but are decidedly confused about how to go about obtaining those results for their own children. Is a 'good' education solely defined by good results in exams? I would venture the view that for many parents this is the whole point of education. Some of the more enlightened parents may give lip service to sport and music and drama, even psychological and emotional health, but grades are writ large in their minds, for grades are stark and crude and bold in their assessment of a child. However, you can't measure well-being in terms of A*s or Cs. Academic grades alone constitute the bottom line.

What is helpful for this discussion is to highlight the difference between 'schooling' and 'education'. Schooling is something that takes place specifically between the ages of five and eighteen, more often than not within a muddle of buildings that contain classrooms and, with any luck, a refectory and a gym. Education is a less tangible business, something in which, if we are lucky, we are engaged throughout the whole course of our lives, mostly wittingly but frequently not. The usefulness of this separation is that it transfers the responsibility for providing education (defined in its broadest sense) from the school alone onto all adults, and especially parents.

Before I elaborate on the implications of this, I want to return to what is a central theme of this book: that is, preparation for adulthood. Is it enough for us just to say that we want our teenagers to be happy and get good academic results? As they come to the business end of their childhood, is it not necessary for us to have a clearer idea of what qualities a fledgling adult might need in order to stand him or her in good stead for adulthood proper?

- Teenagers need to develop the capacity for perseverance in the face of adversity. In other words they need to develop the critically important quality of resilience. This is important because it builds self-esteem and character.

- They need to be able to manage disappointment and failure. We cannot guarantee that they will be successful but we can be sure that at some point in their life they will have to deal with failure. They will certainly learn more from these experiences than they will from their successes.
- They need to be able to make and sustain good relationships because we know without doubt that this capacity is key to having a long and fulfilling life.
- They need to be able to think for themselves and to have confidence in that thinking.
- They need to be able to say and stand by what they believe in, even if others may not agree with it and/or be upset by it.
- They need to be curious about the world.

You are doubtless able to add several more to this list but promoting even these vital qualities in their pupils is often beyond the remit of many schools. Try as they might, their priority is the prescription of curriculum and league tables and more measurable 'outcomes'. So it is, instead, our job, as parents, to make sure we do the best we can to instil these life skills into our children.

Below are a few guidelines and questions, which might ease the way through this tricky task. Let's first be clear what education *doesn't* do:

- It doesn't guarantee that your child will land his or her dream job.
- It will not help them sustain a relationship with friends or a partner.
- It will not insure your child against life's disappointments.

If your children come from a middle class family with two educated parents, then they will have an excellent chance of going to a good university. For a particular social and educational group this is more or less a done deal before the child even makes it through the nursery gates. In this changing world, though, does a university education confer quite the cachet that it used to? Currently one in ten graduates are still unemployed six months after getting their degree and a third of graduates are employed in jobs that don't require one anyway.

Despite the school's exhortations regarding effort and achievement, your child needs to be at the top of his or her game between the ages of 17 and 18. I say this in the hope that parents relax a little if things go haywire for a while. Your child might have more pressing issues to deal with at the ages of six and nine than worrying about academic achievement – issues such as developing their social skills in a group, learning to make friends and following their passions.

Children don't all learn at the same speed and nor is learning a linear process. Becoming caught up in what other children are achieving is a source of pointless angst for parents. Children born in July, for example, are almost a full year behind those classmates born in September. In the early years this can be a significant disadvantage.

Beware of pushing your child too hard. Most of us want our children to do well at school, although I would suggest not always for the right reasons. Unrealistic expectations by parents can create an environment in which the child fears failure knowing that it will hugely disappoint their parents. They need to be self-motivated. The really important grade is the effort grade not the achievement grade. Try not to get seduced by the achievement grade.

Calvin Coolidge Jr, the 30th American president, wrote these wise words:

> Press on. Nothing in the world can take the place of persistence. Talent will not; nothing is more common than unsuccessful men with talent. Genius will not; unrewarded genius is almost a proverb. Education will not; the world is full of educated derelicts. Persistence and determination alone are omnipotent.

Achievement versus Effort

Tom is in his final year of university and is anxious that he will fail his exams. He has some form in this department. He flunked his second year ones and had to retake them. His parents are worried about him, and rightly so. He arrives at my consulting room looking dishevelled and completely unfocused. His jeans look as though they haven't been washed since he bought them and his hair is straggly, greasy and unkempt. His trainers are filthy. He looks a complete and utter mess. But once the meeting starts, I see an altogether different young man beneath the mess. He's bright, insightful, funny and clearly intelligent. We discuss his academic work. He tells me he knows he has to pull his finger out but he just can't get down to the work.

'Have you always had trouble getting down to work, Tom?' I ask.

'Well, I have never really needed to. I always got quite good grades at school. I mean, they weren't special but they were okay. To be honest I was pretty disappointed in the end, I could have done a lot better. I get distracted so easily.'

'Did anyone get on to you about your work? I mean, you were obviously underperforming in a way.'

'No, not really. I was pretty good at knowing how to do the bare minimum without attracting attention. I would throw in the odd A+ essay and that kept everyone off my back. I guess you could say I was just coasting.'

When I explore further, I discover that Tom is one of those adolescents who seems to have slipped under the radar. He didn't try out for any school sports teams although he enjoyed games; he didn't become involved in drama or music productions either. I ask him about holiday work. He says he did the occasional day but nothing substantial. He seems to have gone through the whole schooling process neither succeeding nor failing.

His parents are delightful. He is a much-loved eldest son and as far as I can understand they have provided a stable, loving family life. They are thoughtful and psychologically astute. They have given Tom as much support as they can through the years and are completely at a loss as to how it has come to this crisis point. So what has gone wrong? You might simplistically describe Tom as lazy and unmotivated, and he certainly looks it, but he later reveals what really lies behind this lack of effort: a chronic fear of failure.

Tom is one of those adolescents who is wedded to the idea that he could have been a contender. But his commitment to mediocrity is – typical of many young people – his insurance against his fear of failure. Alongside average grades, Tom consoles himself in his mind that if he tried harder, he would have done really well. He has never given anything his all, so of course he cannot be sure this is the case but it is a reassuring theory. He is outwardly confident and charming. He talks a good game but, beneath the veneer of competence and charm, he is frightened. He is frightened that he doesn't have what it takes to make a success of the next phase of his life. This somewhat Faustian deal with himself has left Tom ill-equipped to deal with the adult challenges that lie ahead. With his finals approaching, he is only too aware that he is probably going to experience his first brush with real failure, something he has successfully managed to evade all his life. But what a time to experience it!

'I'm not really sure I even want to be at university,' he opines.

'Really? And it's taken you until your third year to come to that conclusion?' I ask.

'Well, I never really gave any thought to university or the subject I would study. I just drifted into it.'

'Look, Tom, that ship sailed a while ago. You are beginning your third year, you need to pull your finger out. Now's not the time to be speculating about what you might or might not have done. You just need to get the work done.'

'It's all so boring and pointless. I was reading that lots of young adults with degrees are unemployed so I've been questioning whether there is any point in continuing.'

'Tom, this is all about your fear of failing. If you don't get the work done, it becomes a self-fulfilling prophecy.'

Tom just stares back at me with a helpless look on his face.

I feel like picking him up and shaking him. It's a response to my inability to get him moving. There is an important building block missing in Tom and I'm not sure therapy is the place to find it. What Tom needs is a crash course in putting in effort and dealing with failure, but such courses don't exist and certainly not in the final year of a university degree course.

Tom's story has a familiar ring to it. His parents had unwittingly allowed themselves to be duped by the achievement grades. They are caring parents, but they have handed over the education of their son to the school, lock, stock and barrel. They have left it to them to sort out what is and isn't needed. Tom gained good enough grades throughout his school life and did well enough to make it to university, so from the school's point of view it was a job well done. The crucial question of his effort grades was never addressed. No one bothered to ask why he was coasting and what they might do about it. It is doubtful whether giving Tom a good talking to would have made any difference because the core factor underlying good effort grades is the child's capacity to tolerate or risk failure (in the relative sense). By the time Tom had made it to senior school, his avoidance of effort and commitment, driven by his fear of failure, had become for him a well-established system, and a pretty effective one at that. But it couldn't last.

Tom panicked in the weeks leading up to his finals and failed them. It was a tragedy of sorts, but to my mind Tom was heading for more serious disappointments and failures. I could easily imagine him as one of those adults who is chronically dissatisfied, envious and disparaging of others and their successes, adults who view the achievements of those around them as a combination of luck and opportunity rather than the result of hard work.

From what I understand Tom eventually managed to land a job after months of prevarication and procrastination. I don't think it was what he was expecting but at least it was a start. Now he is up and running everything is still to play for.

Achievement grades are what we parents invariably look at, if we are honest. Good ones reassure us that our child is clever and on track to do well. They are something we can easily boast about – subtly, or not so subtly – to other parents, but they are an illusion. This is because, on the whole, good grades are a reflection of a child's innate ability. Chances are a bright child will pull off a smattering of As, and a super smart one will score even more highly. Eventually, though, most children will hit the glass ceiling, especially in later adolescence, and this is where effort comes into play, as my story about Billy so vividly illustrates.

Professor James Heckman, the Nobel laureate economist at the University of Chicago, has done some interesting research on this issue. He has been gathering evidence which supports the view that how well children manage themselves – as displayed by their persistence towards their goals and other non-academic achievements – predicts their life outcome every bit as much as their IQ.

It is true that some children are more susceptible to this issue than others, but it is the parents' responsibility to address it and not the schools'. You cannot instil this commitment into a three-year-old because younger children need to succeed in various aspects of their lives in order to build up a reservoir of confidence in their own ability. Yet by the age of seven or eight, the connection between effort and achievement has to start to be inculcated. Children need to develop 'stickability' in primary school. This is not always easy because no young child likes to struggle and fail, and neither do their parents like to witness it, so at the very least there will be a measure of resistance and upset. What children usually say is that they don't enjoy an activity anymore, which is often short hand for finding it difficult. It doesn't always have to be piano or the violin; there are a thousand activities out there from ice-skating to rock climbing. You don't have to instil Olympian effort levels, but you do have to make sure they see the project through. If they have signed up to a term of choir or karate, they must not bail out because it proves to be too difficult or 'boring' after all. It is worth reminding yourselves that by committing your child to seeing things through, you are working against the dubious zeitgeist, which has it that everything worth having can be had instantly. Solitarily bucking that trend is necessarily going to be an uphill struggle.

So what happens to the children who reach adolescence without 'stickability' in their locker? Is there anything we can do? Or, to put it another way, how will we know whether they have it or not? There are several general behaviours which attest to the fact that we need to pay attention. One is the appearance of avoidant behaviours, such as leaving work until the last minute, moving or attempting to move the goalposts, poor organisation and philosophical questioning about the value of the project. Another is a general withdrawal from activities towards 'things they can do in their bedroom'.

The answer to the question about what action to take partly depends on the age of the adolescent. The younger they are the easier it is to change things. Here are three important tips:

1. Create a work framework (see page 181 for an example). It should have a specified time period and specified consequences for not completing the work.
2. Don't do deals and don't move the goalposts. Teenagers are experts in trying to avoid reality checks and the two main ways they try to do it is by moving the goalposts and doing deals. It creates an illusion that they are in control of the world. So don't bribe them with money or favours, and don't offer incentives.
3. Don't deliver guilt trips – your child already knows they are messing up, they need strategies for going forward.

The 'Failing' Adolescent

Harry is a young 14. Adolescence has started but he hasn't yet morphed into the more familiar truculent renegade we associate with adolescence. He is still a little soldier mostly doing what he is told. He goes to a very competitive school and his parents are on the sane side of pushy. They are immaculately turned out and they both have a purposeful air about them. You get the picture of a high achieving family. I don't get the impression that they are overbearing but they do expect him to do well. Although Harry does well at school he bombs at exam time. The school says he works himself up into such a state that he can't think. During his end of year tests he had a panic attack and had to leave the classroom. The school suggests he comes to see me to see if I can help him with his panic.

Harry was very reluctant to come and see me. It required much arm-twisting from his parents to get him in. His parents described him as sensitive, shy, quite a perfectionist and prone to withdrawal. Once in the consulting room, I could see how extremely tense and anxious he was. He fiddled and tapped his feet nervously throughout the meeting. His answers to my questions were monosyllabic and there was no attempt by Harry to grasp any of the olive branches I offered. The meeting quickly took on the feel of a police interrogation. There seemed to be a competition developing between us. I was trying to get him to think and engage, and he was steadfast in his refusal to do so. Eventually I capitulated.

'Looks like you've won, Harry, I give up. There's not much point in us continuing this meeting if you're not going to get involved.'

He looked bewildered and then I noticed the slightest of smiles.

'You like to win don't you, Harry?' I asked.

'Yes, I do, I'm a really bad loser.'

At last I seemed to have Harry's attention.

'Is that why exams freak you out? You know, you can't be sure whether you are going to win or not?'

There was a long silence and I wasn't sure he was going to speak.

'Yes, I start thinking about how all the others are doing and if they will get better results than me, then I begin to panic and my mind goes blank. My parents say they are not worried about how well I do, but I know they are.'

For children like Harry, their self-esteem has become inextricably entwined with their exams results and the need to please their parents. This has to be disentangled as soon as possible.

> **H**aving one's personality and self-worth so closely tied up with success is asking for trouble.

We had a family meeting and I put Harry's concerns on the table. He bravely articulated his fear that he might let them down by not doing well and we discussed how much of his sense of self was tied up with winning and how this affected his work. From a psychological point of view you might think of Harry as having a sporting mentality. A mentality that has at its core the idea that first is everything and second is nothing. In a 14-year-old boy this might translate into: 'When I win you love me, and when I don't, you don't love me.'

During the course of the meeting it emerged that Harry was a reasonably talented tennis player but opted out of playing boys who were better or more talented. His parents hadn't taken much notice of this but we identified tennis as something that would help him with his exam panic. We all agreed that he had to play these other boys and take his chances. The thinking behind this idea was that through playing tennis he would develop a more rounded view of winning and losing. I agreed to see him and his parents fortnightly to sort out the issue of their expectations and Harry's understanding of them.

The first fortnight was awful, according to his parents. Harry took a beating in his first match and refused to play anyone else, but his parents wouldn't let him back out. This was difficult as Harry wrongly interpreted their insistence on him playing as putting him under pressure to perform. He played the next few matches without enjoyment or effort and got badly beaten. But over the course of time, things picked up. It became apparent that he was starting to enjoy playing rather than being fixated solely on the result. Almost without noticing it, Harry began to see that life continued as normal despite him losing or winning tennis matches.

My own work with Harry followed a different path. For boys with Harry's problem all relationships and interactions are a form of competition. They like to be first in the dinner queue at school, have more food on their plate than anyone else and they always need to be in charge of the TV remote control. Interactions with siblings and friends are often edgy and competitive. Harry is the second boy in a family and he has two younger sisters. He is sandwiched in the middle and what he is really competing for is his mother's attention. In his mind winning is synonymous with defeating his siblings in his quest to be his mother's favourite.

Over the weeks I manage to unlock this dynamic and bring it closer to home and family life. As the second boy Harry is in fierce competition with his elder brother who is two years older and more accomplished at practically every-thing. This grates with Harry and he often feels hopeless in his efforts to outperform him. He cannot answer the ques-tion as to why he needs to view himself and his life through the prism of his brother's achievements but he acknowledges that he does. There is another important side effect here; Harry's elder brother's ghost comes alive in the form of all the other boys in Harry's peer group. To a lesser or greater extent every one of them comes to represent the elder brother.

It takes time for Harry to process this and start to disen-tangle himself from this complex and distorted world view but eventually he does and when he does we see a very different boy. His sensitivity, his shyness, his anxiety were initially perceived by his parents as character traits but were in fact manifestations of his difficulties. Once the difficul-ties were resolved the shyness disappeared, the anxiety went and he became an altogether more confident boy.

Our understanding of the notion of failure and of failing children is one-dimensional. These young people are vari-ously described as feckless or lazy. Our own, often painful, memories of failure tend to block us from engaging effec-tively with this tricky issue at a time when our children really need us to be on hand to help them through it. What this means is that we are not confronting and dealing with something that will almost certainly have a significant effect on their personality and their attitude to life.

How many times do we hear that so-and-so doesn't try? Lack of effort has a purpose, however perverse that may seem. Not trying is the equivalent of an each-way bet. The reason is that you can hold on to the fantasy that you would have won if you had put in your best effort, but the inevitable outcome, or 'failure', which arises from not trying is not a true indicator of your worth.

We need to look a lot more closely at what goes on in the mind of the failing adolescent rather than reach for the easy clichés. Does failure mean the adolescent sees himself as a failure? Is the experience of failure so damaging that it changes his attitude to the world around him? What is true is that failure and rejection hit all children hard. It is precisely why we often massage reality to soften the blow, and precisely why we shouldn't.

When failure and rejection collide with self-worth, there will be some kind of fallout. This is where we parents need to intervene. Helping the adolescent process this painful experience needs careful and sensitive handling. Don't for one minute believe the mantra, 'I'm not really bothered.' What is critical here as a parent is to gauge the level of 'shock' and that depends on knowing your teenager. For some, not getting a part in the school play is water off of a duck's back but for others it cuts very deep and disturbs their sense of self. Don't make a judgement on the basis of how you would react but on how they react. If they start telling you how they didn't really want the part and the play isn't much good anyway you can bet they feel cut to the quick. Getting them to own up to their disappointment is the first stage. The next is to devise a way forward. Do they need to practice more? Would they like to join a drama group? Empathy without a strategy for going forward isn't much use.

Over the years I have seen dozens of adolescents for whom failure has meant they regard themselves as worthless and their attitude to the world is warped. What links each outcome is the notion that the adolescent has suffered a kind of 'mortal wound', that the experience has penetrated the core of his being, and it is one from which he may never recover.

We know failure is a rite of passage of sorts. Every child has to go through it. We want life to be fair to our children although we know it is not. We know that if they are able to deal effectively with failure it will help build their character and make them more resilient to the ups and downs of life. Conversely, a childhood without any failure isn't much use in adulthood. We all know of school heroes for whom childhood was charmed and the ups and joys came all too easily, and who have lost their way in adulthood, who have crashed and burned and 'failed' spectacularly, with broken marriages, unsatisfactory work, nervous breakdowns, depression, and so on. And indeed those who 'failed' monstrously at school but who have gone on to lead enormously successful lives in terms of work, relationships and the rest. The lists are endless!

Building confidence

So how can we as parents help? In order for adolescents to develop solid self-esteem and character they need not to be afraid of the challenges that life presents; nervous, yes, maybe, but not afraid. We need to keep in mind how our teen approaches these challenges. Naturally most children don't like to fail and it is important that we help them overcome and manage their anxiety. Reluctance to try has several causes as I have outlined above. What we need to do is to gauge what's behind the anxiety as they cannot always do it on their own. If you feel that fear of failure is the major cause then you have to spend some time discussing this with them. Not participating because of fear of failure corrodes self-esteem as the adolescent comes to resent their lack of courage. Paradoxically teenagers who are particularly sensitive to failure need more challenges, not fewer, as long as they are manageable ones. This will build up their confidence.

What do I mean by this in a practical sense? Most schools offer any number of challenges; sporting, musical and artistic to name but a few. All of these activities offer arenas where teenagers can test themselves, where successes and failures can be experienced, where character can be built. If there is nothing at school then something can be found outside of school. This means we have a simple question to ask. Is my teenager engaged in any of the above and if not why not? It is not good enough for them to say 'It's all too boring.' What they really mean is that they are frightened of the psychological rough and tumble that comes with being involved with activities. Of course every teen is different, and they may not enjoy drama or sport; but if they aren't engaged in *anything* then they aren't taking on challenges.

Some adolescents experience abnormally high levels of anxiety in the face of challenges. It paralyses or panics them to such an extent that they invariably fail the test. Timidity and lack of confidence are not the core issues here. Contrary to appearances, these adolescents are internally very competitive. Their issue is that they have to win. It is not enough for them to overcome the challenge. They must, in their minds, be better than everyone else.

Why 'tiger parenting' doesn't work

This neatly leads us into the controversial territory of so-called 'tiger parenting'. What I have just written is fundamentally different from, and even diametrically opposite to, the ideas proposed by the advocates of tiger parenting. Making your child practise the piano, or anything else for that matter, for excessively long periods, is the tiger parent's mantra. This recommendation needs deconstructing.

A number of critical questions come to mind: What kind of parent would subject their child to such a regime? What would be the purpose of such a regime? What kind of child would accept such a regime? And what kind of person might emerge from such an experience? All of the above are worth reflecting upon, but the central question is who is the child doing it for? Is it to please his parents or because he feels passionately about the activity himself? It is worth reminding ourselves that we tend to discover for ourselves the real and meaningful passions in our lives. Rarely do the ones prescribed to us by our parents or teachers become the loves of our lives.

So, back to the regime, are the tiger parent's children practising because they want to and taking pleasure from it, or are they doing so because they want to please (or appease) their parents? The answer to these questions is central to our understanding of what we might want for our children in the future. In other words, there is obedience, servitude and plenty of 'achievement' in the tiger parent regime but very little meaning, wonderment, curiosity, imagination or independent thinking.

The problem with the tiger parent regime – if your child survives it, that is – is that their achievements are in the service of others and are not a result of any sense of self-discovery or self-initiation. The price the so-called 'successful' young adult pays for a lifetime of dancing to someone else's tune is a certain sense of emptiness allied to a lack of curiosity and, often, a chronic inability to initiate and run their own lives. All children, teenagers included, enjoy pleasing us. However, it's more important they engage with activities first and foremost because it gives them pleasure and satisfaction. By all means support their endeavours but don't let your own hopes and wishes get mixed up with theirs.

Over the last few years I have become aware of a new problem affecting older adolescents. Despite being incredibly well schooled they are in point of fact poorly educated. The result is that despite their excellent grades they don't have any of the qualities needed to make a success of adulthood. Whatever you do about schooling you need to pay closer attention to what your children need to be adults.

Top Tips

- **Concentrate on whether your teenager is putting in his best effort, don't get hung up on his attainment grades.**
  Do a little digging around if he's not putting effort in. It's invariably due to a fear of failure and a lack of confidence. You need to support them rather than give them a lecture on how useless and lazy they are.

- **I know it's almost impossible to keep your own hopes and expectations out of the schooling process but do try.**
  You don't want your child to be carrying the burden of your expectations on top of their own.

- **Don't panic at their failures; it's all relative.**
  In 20 years no one will care about their GCSE results. What will matter in 20 years, though, is how they have responded to their failures and disappointments.

- **There is an inverse relationship between their inner confidence and their outer confidence.**
  Teenage confidence is paper thin – don't be fooled into thinking swagger and bravado reflect confidence. Real confidence is hard won through time.

- **If you feel that you have to intervene then make it clear what is expected and structure your intervention accordingly.**
  They need a plan to get from A to B. A general ramble about not working or a lecture about laziness will not be of any help.

CHAPTER 11

Teenagers and Divorce

Forty-two per cent of marriages in the UK end in divorce. More than one in three children will, by the age of sixteen, experience the divorce of their mother and father. Many of these children will face multiple changes of family structure as their parents make relationships with other partners. Many will be exposed to long periods of parental conflict during and after the break up. All this upheaval will undoubtedly have an adverse impact on these children's lives; in some circumstances that impact may resonate well into adulthood.

Elliot is 14 and a real little soldier. He's small, wiry and, in some ways, old beyond his years. It's a quality I have seen in many children of divorced parents. I have been seeing him once a week for a year. His parents divorced nearly two years ago but they are still at war in a low-key sort of way. Arranging dates and events is always fraught with tension, sometimes erupting into full-blown arguments.

Dad has met and married a woman in the intervening period. She has two children of her own from her first marriage, and she is now four months pregnant with a third. They live about an hour away from Elliot's mother and, every other weekend, Elliot travels by train on Friday after school to stay with his father and the new family. His father is preoccupied and excited with his new life and new family. He wants Elliot to be as excited and can't quite acknowledge that it is a struggle for Elliot to absorb so many changes. As a consequence Elliot's relationship with his father has become more distant. When they do see each other, Elliot has to share him with his step-brothers who are much younger.

Elliot says their needs take priority and he feels side-lined. His stepmother is constantly nagging him and he doesn't like her very much. He is resentful of her interfer-ence. He tells me she is not his mother and doesn't have the right to tell him what to do. The weekends at his father's house are not fun and Elliot wonders aloud how long he will have to keep going.

When Elliot arrives home after the weekend, his mother pumps him for information about Dad and his new life. Elliot would like to tell her how he really feels about the weekends but he doesn't in case it creates ill feeling between her and his dad. He says he thinks his mother is lonely and still misses his father. He wants to go out with his friends at the weekend but he feels guilty. He is torn between staying at home with her and getting on with his own life.

'I'm stuck in the middle of two lives and neither of them is much good,' he says. 'I can't wait to get out.'

Sadly, this is an all too familiar story of children with divorced parents.

One day at school Elliot had a meltdown and told his form teacher how miserable he was. The school was sufficiently worried to refer him to therapy. Elliot's life is not awful on a day-to-day basis, far from it, but he is stressed out managing the whole complex of different homes and new relationships on top of his own burgeoning adolescence. He says he dreams of going to university and that, when he does, he won't go back home.

I hear Elliot's story far too often. On the surface, despite a bit of tension, there is an organised, civilised arrangement in place. However, the living of it is hard work and takes its toll. It is draining dealing with all the changes and new relationships. Eventually something has to give, although in what way is not yet clear. Elliot is in the throes of adolescence and has a lot of psychological work to do. So far he is not doing it. It is as much as he can do to manage his complex set of living arrangements.

In my opinion there is no such thing as an amicable divorce, at least as far as the children are concerned. There are just degrees of awfulness. It is possible to mediate the awfulness – as Elliot's parents have done to a certain extent – but the harsh truth is that, however attentive and grown-up a separating pair may be, they cannot eliminate it entirely. What is manageable for a child at the age of eight, may not be manageable for her at sixteen. In other words, the experience of divorce means different things and presents different problems to children at different ages. It is impossible to make a judgement about how successful parents have been at dealing with the fallout until the child reaches adulthood. This is not to suggest that I am condemning parents who decide to divorce. On the contrary, an awful marriage can be equally, if not more, damaging for children. What I am challenging is the notion that for children it is ever pain free. Just because they are getting on with their lives without breaking down every week does not mean they are fine. What it means is they are, like Elliot, coping.

So what is it exactly that Elliot is dealing with?

- Two different homes
- Two stepbrothers
- A new baby on the way
- A woman who is not his mother telling him what to do
- A mother who is lonely and for whom he often feels responsible
- Having to share his father
- Adolescence

That is a pretty hefty psychological package for a 14-year-old. The point about Elliot's story is that, on the scale of divorce horror stories, it is actually not too bad. His parents have agreed an access arrangement that works, more or less; they don't fight openly; and life is fairly civilised at both ends. But for Elliot, juggling his varied logistical arrangements and his complicated and conflicting emotions, life at times seems nigh on impossible.

What comes across in the sessions is the sense of Elliot feeling completely overwhelmed. There is so much to think about he doesn't know where to start. I try and break it down for him but I can see that he can't summon up the wherewithal to get on top of any of it. Is it any wonder he has had meltdowns at school?

I realise that what he needs from me is not to make any demands on him. He wants a quiet space just to be. For the first months we speak about the small things in his life – his friends, TV. They seem trivial in the grand scheme of things, but they are 'his things'. Gradually he begins to unpack all the confusions and frustrations. In one sense they are all mini traumas that need to be processed: Dad and Mum breaking up; Dad moving to a new home; Dad and his new partner; new step-siblings, etc. Underpinning all of this is an intense feeling of anger that this is not the life he wants to be living. There is a sort of grieving that he needs to go through, a grieving for the old life he used to lead, a process that has to precede the living of the new life.

Elliot made slow and steady progress. He couldn't pinpoint the moment when he felt better about life but gradually he did. He made a good group of friends and began to separate himself from his family. The game changer was his decision not to go and see his father on alternate weekends. It took him weeks to pluck up the courage to speak to him. His father was at first angry but then heartbroken. He was close to tears when he rang me to ask what to do. Elliot's reasoning was that he didn't want to spend alternate weekends away from his friends. He was now 15 going on 16, and his social life was developing rapidly. He didn't know anybody where his father lived. His father knew that there wasn't much he could do about Elliot's decision. I tried to reassure him that this might only be a temporary state of affairs and that things could change in the future. In many ways Elliot's father was going to have to deal with exactly what Elliot had years earlier, to live a life he hadn't signed up to. I wondered whether Elliot was indulging in a bit of payback. Once Elliot had brokered these changes he quickly stopped coming to see me. I didn't try to force the issue. I am sure there is still a lot of work for him to do but for the time being he rightly wants to get on with his life.

It remains to be seen how Elliot copes as he gets older because divorce means different things to children at different times in their lives. Whatever arrangements are made they are nearly always at some cost one way or another. What seems critical to the child's development is their capacity to live with the psychological consequences of that cost.

I want to take a look at the various aspects of divorce – the break up, access arrangements, step parenting and other issues, and try and outline what we can do as parents to mediate the more damaging aspects of the process. I realise that every divorce is different but there are some general points that are worth holding in mind.

The Break Up

When marriages break up parents know how hard it is going to be for their children, but they have to defend themselves against that pain. The way they usually do it is to focus, obsessively sometimes, on what and how to tell the children. This preoccupation with what, how and when is perfectly understandable, but it avoids consideration of the bigger picture. It gives the impression, wrongly, that if you get the initial conversation right, the break up will be less painful. The truth is that the initial conversation just sets a process in motion, nothing more. The process will need addressing in different ways at different times throughout childhood and adolescence, and it is ongoing.

I am not sure that the 'when' to tell them matters very much. Naturally and quite rightly you want them to have some time to process what might – or might not – be shocking news. Adolescents are far more perceptive than we give them credit for. They can sense when something is not right at home. Hearing that Mum and Dad are breaking up may merely serve to confirm what they already knew intuitively. It doesn't make the problem of dealing with the break up easier, but it may not be quite the total shocker parents imagine.

The 'what' to tell them is more complex and depends to a large extent on the age of the child. Younger children don't have the conceptual framework to understand long and convoluted explanations as to why their mother and father are splitting up.

It is different with adolescents. As a general rule, it is better to give a simple and straightforward explanation along the lines of, 'We have not been getting on and don't love each other in the way a couple should any longer, so we have sadly decided to part. We're going to try to make the change as easy as possible for you guys and we will always love you.' This covers the necessary bases and sets the process in motion. You may want to add or subtract bits to the above but whatever you do, do not under any circumstances start blaming one another and do not even think about going into the gory details. Remember, at this stage, it is not about you; it is about helping your adolescent manage difficult and upsetting information.

What makes divorce especially complex for teenagers is that as part of a normal developmental process they are trying to separate themselves from their parents. This complex and often upsetting process is the reason so many teenagers go to war with their parents. If their parents are engaged in their own war to separate it can interfere with this important developmental process.

They will of course react in different ways; some with tears, some with anger, some with indifference. For most, it takes a considerable while to absorb the shock and even longer to understand what it means. Appearances can be deceptive. Refrain from falling into the trap of believing that, because your teenager seems to be taking it in their stride, they are somehow fine with their new circumstances. That may make you feel better but they are merely managing, I am afraid to say, no more than that. There is no scope for complacency. If they don't voluntarily talk about how they are feeling, you can give them a little nudge from time to time by way of asking them how they are coping. Some of their answers may surprise you.

What is beyond doubt is that the occasion when you tell the children you are getting divorced is very decidedly not to be seen as an opportunity for point scoring or mud-slinging with your erstwhile spouse. (In fact, at no point must you ever go in for such damaging behaviour.) I realise this is easier said than done, especially when feelings are running as high as they necessarily will be. But sticking to this simple explanation is enough to initiate a process that may take many months and even years for your children to fully understand. However you couch it, adolescents will want more explanation and are likely to take a view which will be quite black and white. It is also possible that you may not like what you hear. I would strongly advise that you do not become drawn into a dialogue that tries to locate the blame with one parent or the other. By all means listen to your child's grievances, if that is what they are, but stay away from judgements and condemnation. Establishing the truth of why a marriage breaks down is a complex business. Adolescents don't have the life experience to grasp much more than basic explanations. Understanding how a marriage breaks up takes most children years to resolve. The questions that it raises cannot be resolved with one dialogue, so don't try.

My suggestions are not always well received. If one partner wants the marriage to stay intact and the other does not, the one who does will tell me that they don't want to lie to their teenager, they think he or she should know the truth. I understand this point of view, but it immediately places the spouse who wants to end the marriage in the dock and makes him or her the villain. This parent can become the object of the children's anger but this is not helpful to anybody in the longer term.

Speaking of truth, it is worth remembering that a marriage break up is a joint venture. Husband and wife, if not entirely equal in terms of responsibility, both definitely play a part, to a greater or lesser degree. The fact that one or other of them may have taken a sledgehammer to the marriage in a thoroughly unpleasant fashion, is the final act in what has more often than not been a long and perhaps slow disintegration. If you really want to learn something from a divorce – and by that I mean psychologically – then focus on what you yourself may have contributed to it as opposed to only on how aggrieved you feel. You will learn nothing from the misplaced fancy that you are a wholly innocent victim.

So, having set the ball rolling, what happens next? How things pan out from here on in depends a great deal on whether the break up is an amicable or hostile one. It is fairly obvious that if a couple both come to the view that the marriage is over, it is more likely that they will be able to keep the children in mind and help them through the difficult transition. Most of the post-divorce parenting guides that I have read are only relevant for parents who go through amicable break ups. All the do's and don'ts only make sense when there is a degree of amicability between the couple.

The acrimonious divorce is about as difficult and unpleasant an experience as any adult or child is likely to go through. It is both extraordinary and tragic that a couple that sets out with love, trust and hope can end up behaving with such manifest selfishness, bitterness and cruelty wrapped up in the thick and unbecoming coating of self-righteousness. If you recognise yourself here, be aware that by the time you have extracted your pound of flesh from your partner, your behaviour and the fallout from it will have left an indelible imprint on your teenager's memory; memories that may disturb them for many years to come. Just because you are no longer husband and wife, you still have responsibilities as a parent, and part of that responsibility is to protect your child from as much of the fallout as you can. Those couples engaged in a variation of a fight to the death, are not attending properly to the children. Signing them up to ride shotgun on your crusade to seek revenge, or so-called justice, causes children and adolescents huge amounts of pain.

Access Arrangements

The next hurdle to face parents is who gets the kids and when? It is not surprising, given the trauma of divorce, that parents often seem to overlook the fact that breaking up means you lose your children for part or all of the week. This sudden realisation can set the scene for another bloody battle about who has the children and when. Fathers, who have never changed a nappy and work all hours, suddenly begin asking to have their two-year-old for half the week. Mothers magically arrive at the notion that their children don't need to see their father apart from every other Saturday. The negotiation surrounding such critical questions can become nothing short of a tragedy when parents start squabbling over their children as if they are objects to be traded. The bottom line is that children need both their parents, however useless you may feel the other one is or however angry you feel with your ex.

There is a fundamental misunderstanding at the heart of this matter. For couples with children, divorce is another kind of marriage. You may well no longer want or need to have much to do with each other after divorce, but the children bind you until they are young adults, and often beyond. This matters because, however much you dislike your co-parent, however much you regret ever having met them in the first place, however much you hate them, you are going to have to find a way of communicating and working with them, in the interest of your children's well-being.

This is so easy to write down here, or to tell my clients, but so monumentally difficult in practice. One client told me she knew restraint was all-important, in fact the only way not to send her children to hell in a handcart. She managed never once to say a word against her ex-husband, but there were times when being restrained felt for her as if she were 'swallowing a two-litre bottle of pure acid which eviscerated my insides'. I would strongly recommend seeing a professional if you cannot sort out a way of working and communicating with your ex. You will save your children from the worst of the fallout of having to deal with your toxic acrimony.

It is stating the obvious to say that access should be an arrangement that has the children's best interests at heart. You would have thought this statement is self-evident, but it is extraordinary how it can be twisted and manipulated by 'concerned' parents. In such situations it seems that the pain of the loss is unbearable, and retaliation and revenge completely blocks out the possibility of sensible discussion about the children's needs.

A father of three young children came to see me ostensibly to ask my opinion on access arrangements. He was a big man in every sense. He ran a successful European company and, like many such men I have seen over the years, he was used to getting his own way. A meeting with these sorts of fathers is not a voyage of discovery – they have already decided the outcome. The only remaining issue is how to get there. His wife was divorcing him and I could see he was in a very distressed, agitated state and was trying hard to cover it up. It quickly became clear that what he was really after was not my opinion but a professional to legitimise his course of action. On the one hand he tried to convey a picture of himself as even-handed and reasonable, but the bitterness and vindictiveness towards his ex-wife was barely disguised. His story quickly descended into mud-slinging, albeit sophisticated mud-slinging. I suspected that help-lessness and rejection were not emotions he could easily digest; he was on a revenge mission disguised as a quest for access advice.

The underlying reason for fighting for 50/50 access was to punish his ex-wife for having the audacity to divorce him and the way he was going to do it was to deprive her of the children. He tried to convince me that he couldn't bear to be without his children for long and that it was only right that he have 50 per cent of the time with them. I pointed out that one of the factors in the divorce was the fact that he travelled a great deal and was hardly ever around, so how was he going to look after the children? He told me that he had all that taken care of but didn't specify what exactly that entailed. Was he going to look after them or get someone else in to take care of them? I pushed hard on this and I could see he didn't like it. I suspected there was nothing organised and that he would just hire nannies and various babysitters to cover the time. He threw in what he believed to be his trump card, an appeal to a greater authority. He would let the court decide. It was, he said, the only way forward. Mediation, he insisted, was a waste of time. Courts are not, in my opinion, always the best places to decide on the welfare of children. In this case the court rejected the father's request for 50/50 access and imposed a more sensible access arrangement. The acrimony and the fallout from it badly impacted on the children. What changed everything for the better was that the father found a new partner who managed to bring some sanity to the proceedings by mediating his aggressive stance. The whole access issue calmed down as a result. Reluctantly he started to work with his ex-wife rather than against her.

Adults whose lives have been blighted by these dysfunctional dynamics as children can spend years trying to resolve the fallout. Relationship issues, self-esteem issues, depression, addictions ... you name it, it's all on the list of possibilities. When you set out on the road of seeking revenge through your children be absolutely clear that you understand the consequences of your actions.

Revenge is not the only factor conspiring to obscure the children's best interests. Divorced parents find the schizophrenic life difficult, especially at the beginning. When the children are around it is noisy, chaotic, lively, exasperating and fun. When they are not, it is mercifully quiet but alarmingly lonely. And while the transitions are difficult enough for adults, what these adults often fail to take into account is the fact that the children have to cope with the peripatetic life as well. What is more, until these children are quite a bit older, they don't have any say in it. This dual existence is foisted upon them and they just have to put up with it.

I made the point earlier that the divorced parents are bound together in some way until their children become young adults. An appreciation of this should help take the sting out of the early access madness. An adolescent girl will need to spend more time with her mother. A teenage boy might well want to spend more time with his father. An older child may ask to go and live with one or other parent because they get on better with one than the other, and/or one lives nearer to school or to friends.

The more entrenched among you might be thinking, 'This is all well and good, but what would you suggest is a good access arrangement?' Generally speaking, I am in favour of there being one central home, usually with the mother, and regular time spent with the father. In practice this means that the children have a base where they can centre themselves as well as enjoy regular time with Dad. The arrangement might look something like this: every other weekend (Friday to Sunday), and one evening a week with Dad. Provided there is flexibility and a degree of cooperation, this shouldn't preclude Dad from taking the children to school or picking them up as the need/desire arises, or indeed taking them out for a pizza if he has the time or they want to see him 'out of hours', as it were.

Why should the central home be with the mother and not the father? I am sure that there are many fathers who could, if pushed, do as good a job of looking after their children as mothers, but it is my contention that it is the centrality of the child's relationship to his or her mother that swings it for me. The maternal relationship is the foundation of a child's development. In normal development the adolescent leaves the maternal relationship. By making the father's home the central one, the mother is in essence forced into leaving the child. It is my view that this has the potential to create abandonment issues for the child.

I am aware that my suggestion raises another important question by dint of omission: why shouldn't the children consider themselves to have two equal bases and have half and half time with each parent, for example, one week with Mum and one with Dad? This all sounds fair and reasonable but it begs a simple question, the answer to which rather blows the idea out of the water, in my view: How would *you* like to live in one place for one week, with one person or group of people, and another the following week? I doubt if many of you would be too keen. This system seems to me to be more about the parents' needs and convenience than the children's. I have to date never met a single child who has liked this system.

Post-Divorce

Once the break up is over and most of the issues between the parents are agreed, if not resolved for good, the peripatetic nature of post-divorce life kicks in. The relief that a painful and often acrimonious process has come to an end is often short-lived as adolescents and parents struggle to become accustomed to the new arrangements. The difficulties in managing the logistics take some getting used to; old wounds and grievances are easily resurrected. It needs patience and understanding to ensure the system works.

The noise and hubbub that accompanies life with the children is now punctuated by longer (or shorter) bouts of silence and loneliness when they are absent. Having lived a life consumed by family and children, ex-partners now have to process the pain of another loss when the children are with the other parent. Weekends can be frittered away waiting for the children to return. In my experience mothers find this more difficult for obvious reasons, especially those who before the divorce gave up careers and work to look after the children.

A question I am frequently asked is: How often should I speak to my children when they are with their father and vice versa? It is an interesting conundrum and not as straightforward as you might imagine. The answer depends on motive. Do you want to speak to your children because you miss them? This is not by itself a good enough reason to call them. Most switched-on children will pick up on your distress; it is your job to contain their worries, not their job to contain yours. Telling them that you are missing them can make them feel guilty about having a good time while they are away from you.

Are you in reality checking up on how they are being looked after? This is often the truth behind a mother who tends to have a controlling nature and it is a bone of contention for many fathers. By and large – feel free to shoot me down – fathers don't look after children as well as mothers on a purely practical level, but this doesn't mean they are going to damage them if they give them endless takeaway pizzas and sit on the sofa watching TV. The glitches are less a result of poor parenting skills, and more that fathers are out of practice and often have too few hours and days with their children, so every moment is precious and they don't want to waste time bogged down by domestic trivia. You will only inflame the fragile post-divorce peace by repeatedly checking up on them.

As for the older adolescent, any intrusion into their world will usually be met with hostility at worst and irritation at best. So don't be offended when your teenager is with your ex-other-half, if you are repeatedly diverted to voicemail.

Changing Relationships

While there is relative calm and a semblance of order to post-divorce family life, it marks the beginning of a new relational order.

Without his father around, 13-year-old Craig is now the man of the house. The space next to Mum on the sofa is empty and Craig is only too ready and eager to fill it. Mum feels lonely in the evening and enjoys the chats with him. She notices how grown-up and responsible he has become. He helps empty the dishwasher and puts the rubbish out, jobs that her ex-husband did when he was around. He has even started telling his siblings what to do, although she would rather he wasn't so rough with his younger brother.

Fifteen-year-old Jean is busy helping her dad in his new flat. She busies herself putting things away and tidying up. Dad is a hopeless cook so she takes over the preparation of food and the feeding of her seven-year-old brother and three-year-old sister. Dad is grateful for the help. It is early days in his post-divorce life and he struggles with managing all three children at once.

On the surface everything is looking pretty good but this is misleading. The new dynamics are confusing for all concerned. Craig seems to have replaced Dad and Jean has replaced her mum. As the months pass, Craig has taken to having a say about more or less everything that goes on in the house and complains bitterly about his siblings' behaviour. His mother has become slightly frightened of him as his tempers have become more volcanic especially when she reprimands him. He is also more aggressive with his siblings. The roughness with his younger brother verges on bullying.

Meanwhile, Jean's helpful persona appears to have disappeared overnight to be replaced by a sulkier, more argumentative self. Dad has a girlfriend and at the weekends when he has the children, he has on occasion asked Jean to babysit the other two while he goes out. Jean agrees but is not happy about this and has been on the phone to her mother complaining about her dad. This has caused tension and arguments between the parents.

The absence of one or other parent from the home creates a job vacancy which the eldest, opposite sex child is initially only too happy to take on. Craig believes that with his father no longer there, he is the man of the house. Jean thought she was Daddy's girl and is furious that she has been passed over in favour of a stranger.

These fictitious vignettes illustrate how mindful divorced parents need to be of the shifting relational landscape. It is important to make sure the children remain children and are not prevailed upon to assume the mantle of the absent partner.

Here are some other do's and don'ts when interacting with your children post-divorce … Don't promise things you can't deliver because you might regret digging yourself into a hole. A familiar one is, 'I promise I'm never going to get married again.' Really? Can you be absolutely sure? Sure as eggs are eggs, a broken promise beckons.

Another is, 'No, we will never move from the family home.' Children want certainty especially after a break up. But the question they are really asking is a very different one. Behind the quest for certainty is a more philosophical plea: 'Please promise me that the world will never change.' This is a promise you cannot deliver, so be careful about definitive statements.

The other route, post-divorce, might go something like this: 'I am not going to have another relationship (for whatever reason). Instead, I am going to devote myself to my children.' Admirable though this may appear on the surface, it implies that you are in effect exchanging a relationship with a partner for a similar relationship with your children. In other words, your children are going to be your new partners. However good and selfless your intentions, this is a project fraught with difficulties. As the children enter adolescence, the process of separation from their parents can become even more problematic than usual if the child realises that his mother is going to be very lonely once he has left home. Do not steer clear from a new relationship for the sake of the children. It may be a rocky road, but it will be far rockier if you have sacrificed your future and put all your eggs in your children's baskets. When they leave home, your own nest is going to feel all the more empty.

New partners

Someone once told me that, for children, sex between their parents is like wallpaper in a room: they see it but they don't notice it. Once you're divorced and dating someone, it is right up there in flashing neon lights. How do you broach this with them? Do you tell them about your new partner or do you keep him or her a secret? And how and when do you introduce the children to your new love interest?

At the outset, there is no need to tell the children anything. This was true when you were married and it is the same now you are divorced. Your private life is your private life. However, for adolescents in the throes of managing their own fledgling sexuality, this is all tricky ground. Their curiosity, allied to an often fundamentalist view, can make this a minefield. Whatever you do, don't fall into the trap of thinking because they are 15 they can handle knowing about your romantic life; they cannot. Although they might pretend they can.

If they ask you whether you have a girlfriend (who may or may not become an important other in your life), you could start by asking them why they want to know. This may help establish initially whether they are interested in you, or they have some other concern in their head. For example, if the answer runs along the lines of, 'Well, Freddie's dad has met someone and is going to move to Australia,' you can glean that they are worried you might do the same. (An appropriate answer to this might be, 'Don't worry guys, that's not going to happen.')

You might, alternatively, be confronted with, 'Dad, I saw your phone and read a message to someone called Joan. Who is Joan?' The knowledge that their mother or father has a new partner inevitably creates anxieties and questions, some of them uncomfortable for you, others just plain embarrassing. However difficult, you must not lie. Be truthful but cut the intimate details.

So: 'Joan is a friend.'

'Are you going out with her?'

'Look guys, I am seeing her and if the relationship becomes important and special, I will tell you.'

Different responses, both spot on. There is nothing wrong with saying you are seeing someone, but you do not need to discuss your sex life and you do not need to go into a lot of detail.

A frequent question I get asked is: 'How and when should I introduce a new partner?' The answer to this question is blindingly obvious and doesn't need a psychologist to spell it out: take it slowly, very slowly. Children take time to get used to someone new in their lives. Relationships need to be tweaked; sex is now on the radar and that takes adolescents a good while to digest.

I have seen many divorced parents, mainly fathers, who know the answer but want to get away with fast-tracking the process. He has a new girlfriend and they are anxious to set up home together as quickly as possible. The question about introducing her to the children has a subtext: once she has been introduced, it can be full steam ahead – new home, she moves in without further ado, whole new order in place, no hanging about. What this father who comes to see me really wants to know is how quickly he can pull this feat off without incurring too much grief from his children. Having gone through a painful divorce – in the sense that they are always, at the very least, stressful – quite why he wants to launch himself at rocket speed into potentially more chaos is one of the mysteries of relational life. I know love is blind, but this seems like jumping off a cliff hoping you land on something soft.

Step-parents

This is a fascinating and immensely challenging area for both adults and children. It is a situation fraught with psychological misunderstandings and deluded hopes. There is something about the step-relationship that causes adults to think and behave in mysterious ways.

A has had an affair with B. A divorces his wife and moves in with B, almost immediately. He has his children at the weekends and insists on introducing them to B. He is completely miffed as to why the children are not exactly overjoyed with this arrangement and B cannot understand why the children seem so hostile.

Here are two stories about the difficulties of integrating new partners into your children's lives.

Andrew is the eldest of three siblings. He is your archetypal teenager, all energy and aggravation. His mother and father divorced five years ago. It wasn't especially acrimonious and the passage of time has eased the painful memories. However, his mother has met someone with whom she hopes to start a long and lasting relationship. She has tried to take the new relationship slowly so that the children might be more accepting, but they are resistant and Andrew is the worst. He doesn't see why he needs to come to me so he's not exactly full of the joys of spring when he arrives for the first consultation.

'It's my mum who needs to be here, not me.'

'You might be right, Andrew, but now you're here why don't we make use of it? You're free to say what you like. From what Mum said to me I gather you're not too happy about her new boyfriend.'

'Well, nor would you be. He's a complete dick. He pretends to be interested in us. He asked me about my homework the other day. I mean, what for? Why is he pretending to care about my homework? It is all so fake. I think it's just to suck up to Mum. He's always trying to be mates and say cool things. It's pathetic. We've only known him a few weeks, yet when he's there he walks around the house like he owns it. The other day he even told me to tidy up my room so I just told him to fuck off. Mum just laughs but it's embarrassing. Why doesn't he act normally instead of being such a try-hard?'

Andrew was right: I did need to see his mother and the meeting with her wasn't an easy one. She was completely resistant to taking on board Andrew's point of view. She wanted her new partner to 'replace' her husband and act as if he was their father. I pointed out that they already had a father and they didn't need another one. I suggested, as Andrew had rightly surmised, that the new partner should just try to be more relaxed around the children. I went further and warned her that the project was doomed to failure if she continued with it in this way. She then told me an important story that perfectly illustrates the complications of step-parenting. Her new partner didn't have any children and had desperately wanted some. For a variety of reasons it hadn't worked out for him. Being with her and her children gave him the perfect opportunity to become the parent he had always wanted to be.

I offered to see them both but the opportunity was declined. He said he had no wish to speak to someone like me and that is how it ended. I wondered from time to time how it had all worked out. My work with children is like reading a good book but with the last chapter missing. I almost never come to know how things turn out, it can be incredibly frustrating.

As coincidence would have it, a year later I bumped into Andrew in the street near where I work. We exchanged an uneasy hello and I asked him how things were. He said fine. I then asked him about his stepfather.

'No, that all finished ages ago, thank God. I think Mum got the message in the end. He was always interfering and trying to be a better parent than my dad. It was pointless really.'

As a step-parent, you will encounter all manner of difficulties with the children if you deliberately set out to parent, cultivate or buy their affection. They will quickly sense that you want something from them and may use it to their advantage.

Bob has been divorced for less than a year. The divorce experience was soul-destroying and exhausting. His three children, aged 12, 14 and 16, suffered a great deal, which was why he came to see me. The children and I did a little work sorting out what they had made of it all. This seemed to settle them and we left it at that.

Bob came to see me again six months later with a very different problem. He had met a woman who he really liked and, after four months' dating, she had moved into his house with the children. Since then it had been chaos. The children hadn't taken to her at all. They either ignored her or were downright rude. What had precipitated the call was that the youngest had cut up one of her expensive dresses and this had resulted in a huge row.

I listened to this story with a certain degree of incredulity. Why had he moved her in after just four months, in fact, why had they moved in together at all? His ex had the children every other weekend, so they were free to have time together without any children and do whatever they wanted. And why did he think his adolescent children would automatically want to make friends with someone they hardly knew? All this, and after having just gone through the hell of a divorce. The relationship with the new partner, he said, was now in doubt after the row about the dress and the children were in open rebellion.

We agreed to have a meeting – Bob, the children and myself – to try and broker peace. The children, still wounded from the divorce, were adamant that they didn't want anyone with them right now although they were okay, just about, with Dad having a girlfriend. Bob listened and reluctantly accepted what they had to say. His new partner moved out. I can't say for sure what happened further down the line but they would have a much better chance of success by taking things slowly.

These are two examples of the all-too-prevalent kind of relational madness that grips parents and their new partners: wildly unrealistic expectations allied to a blatant disregard to how the children feel.

In my experience, the expectations of step-relation-ships and children are far too high. It is less a case of wondering why teenagers' attitudes fluctuate between hostility and indifference, and more why they should be interested in a step-parent at all. In most cases, children already have two parents they love; a third, particularly one they barely know and who is a shadow of their replaced parent, would seem entirely surplus to requirements.

In the short term, if the children tolerate the 'other' without rudeness or bad behaviour, then that is a good outcome. In the longer term, they may grow to like that step-parent and in some cases even love him or her, but note that by the longer term I mean years, not weeks or months.

Below are a few guidelines on step-parenting:

1. Don't try and parent the children unless they ask for it.
2. Stay away from disciplining them unless specifically asked.
3. Don't ingratiate yourself to them through presents or treats. You cannot buy love and respect.
4. Don't tolerate rudeness or disrespectful behaviour directed towards you. Make sure this is dealt with by you as a couple.
5. They will respect you in the long run if you behave in a respectful way towards them.
6. Don't try and compete with or attempt to replace the children's birth parent.

Top Tips

- **While divorce is without doubt difficult for children it doesn't have to be the end of the world if you can manage the break up in a civilised way and keep their needs at the forefront of your mind.**

- **A bitter and acrimonious divorce is a very painful experience for teenagers.**
  The repercussions can last a long time. Being angry with your ex doesn't have to translate into a war with your children. Do everything you can to prevent this.

- **What you tell teenagers is less important than what they make of it.**
  'The truth' matters less than their understanding of what has happened. They will work it out for themselves eventually.

- **When considering access arrangements bear in mind how you would feel living the life you are about to impose on your child.**

- **Do not bad-mouth your ex in front of your teenager under any circumstances.**
  They are not interested.

- **If you are a step-parent keep your expectations low.**
  Teenagers already have two parents. Why would they be interested in another one?

- **Just because teenagers are not breaking down every day, it doesn't mean they are fine with it.**
  It takes a long while for children to process a break up so pay attention and be vigilant.

- **Just because you find another partner who you love and want to share your life with don't expect your teenagers to necessarily share your enthusiasm.**
  Be patient.

D ivorce doesn't have to be traumatic if both parents can remain civil and amicable, but rest assured an acrimonious one most certainly is.

Conclusion: A Tale of Two Teenagers

I receive a desperate call one afternoon from the mother of Josh. She asks me if I remember the family. She tells me she came to see me with her husband about their son, 10 years earlier, when he was 15. I don't immediately remember him but listen carefully to his mother's story. Josh is now 25 and is not in good shape. She asks if she can come in and talk about him and we arrange an appointment for the following day. I dig out the file to refresh my memory.

I see Josh was a difficult but not overly troubled adolescent at that time. He was bright and doing reasonably well at school, although it was clear he was cruising and more comfortable avoiding challenges than taking them on. I note that he had quite an extreme reaction to setbacks. He had been dropped from the school football team and in a fit of pique had refused to play football ever again. This struck me as both puzzling and worrying. His parents confirmed that he showed similar traits at home. Josh could be stubborn and angry if things didn't go his way. The parents had 'accommodated' these characteristics into the fabric of family life to ensure they all had some peace. What this meant in practice was that parenting him involved a series of deals and bribes. However as a truculent 15-year-old even this strategy didn't seem to work for long. I underlined this in my notes and made a comment to the effect that I needed to take this up with them at the meeting.

The meeting a decade earlier had not gone well from the outset. We were at odds over our understanding of Josh's intransigence and even more at odds over what to do about it. I suggested they should stop doing deals and bribing him. The rationale was that we needed to help Josh manage the world he was moving rapidly into, a world where he couldn't do deals to get his own way. I added that this would more than likely present him with more managed setbacks, which we could then work with in order to understand what was going on. The parents, more especially the father, viewed things differently. The gist of his argument was, why create problems and conflict when surely what we needed to be doing was avoiding them? I saw the logic, but countered that not being able to navigate setbacks would be a significant handicap for a young adult.

The child's reaction to the disappointments, rejections and failures in their life provides the template for the more serious teenage and adult setbacks. In early life they can appear relatively insignificant, as in Josh's case, but navigating them successfully builds character and emotional resilience. They need to get over the 'perceived unfairness' and grievance. This requires us to engage with these issues robustly and not let our children back out. Just letting it go often seems the easier option, but don't.

In Josh's case potential setbacks were going to come thick and fast as he got older. If he couldn't manage them now, how on earth was he going to manage them later? His parents were not persuaded and in a way I understood why. It is hard to envisage our teens as adults. It is often a step too far. They did not like the idea of confrontations and arguments as a way of resolving problems. Not many of us enjoy arguments and confrontations but sometimes they are necessary. As adults we have the experience and maturity to know that difficult issues have to be tackled; it is part of being an adult. Our capacity to engage with the difficult stuff is also a sign of how much we care. That adolescents sometimes view these dialogues as an infringement of their human rights is neither here nor there.

I sensed Josh's parents were not going to budge and suggested an accommodation. I offered to see Josh to try to understand a little more about what was going on. They both baulked at the idea. They worried Josh would think there was something wrong with him if they brought him to a 'shrink' and they didn't want him to think he was crazy. No, they wanted to know what to do without bringing him in to see me. I understood their wish for this sort of help but as a way of parenting adolescents it doesn't work because you have to engage them in a process that may take weeks, or longer. They are far too smart to buy into a quick fix especially if it involves them not being able to do what they want. I politely told them that I didn't think I could help them. We ended up agreeing to disagree. That was the last I heard of them until the call from Josh's mother 10 years later.

The day after she rings, she comes to see me and I recognise her instantly. She looks a lot older and as she tells the story it is evident that the intervening years have taken a heavy toll. The story is instructive as well as painful. She describes how they went to see another professional after our unproductive meeting all those years ago, who suggested a much more palatable option. In short, this consisted of positively praising Josh's behaviour and supported the father's view of avoiding/deflecting confrontation at all costs. The professional's opinion was that Josh would grow out of it with time and maturity. According to his mother, this had worked well in the sense that life at home became more settled. Josh did well enough to go to university. He found a girlfriend at the end of his first year and was getting on with his studies. However, in the middle of his third year, it all started to unravel when Josh's girlfriend broke up with him. This setback hit him really hard and seemed to precipitate a decline. He became withdrawn and saw less and less of his friends. He started to neglect his work. Unbeknown to his parents at the time, he also started smoking weed heavily.

Although he was expected to do well at university, in the end he barely scraped a third class degree. He returned home afterwards but remained uncommunicative and cut off. His parents managed to persuade him to apply for some jobs but he was rejected from them all without an interview. This was hardly surprising given his withdrawn state and half-hearted approach. Applying for those jobs was, his mother recounts, the last time he meaningfully ventured out into the real world. Now he spends most of his time in his bedroom playing computer games and smoking weed. Telling me this, she breaks down and sobs. And there is more. She tells me that she can hear him screaming in his bedroom at night sometimes. She wonders if he is hallucinating.

She asks me if I will see Josh. I tell her that the situation is more complex and that he needs to see an adult psychiatrist in the first instance. I tell her that his drug use appears to have become a major problem now. These issues need addressing by an expert in this field before he sees someone like me. I give her the name of a psychiatrist.

As she leaves I ask after her husband. She tells me that the marriage has been under strain for a while. She and her husband argue all the time about their son. She says that they are racked with guilt that they didn't do anything when they had the chance. I try to reassure her that all is not lost and, if they can get Josh to see the psychiatrist, it is possible things can be turned round but they need to force the issue.

Josh's mother called me several weeks later to tell me that they and Josh were feeling much more positive. He had seen a psychiatrist and was making huge efforts to stop smoking weed. Josh was feeling brighter and more energised. He had also agreed to see a therapist, which was another positive sign. I'm hopeful that with time he will get back into life, however his story is a salutary reminder of what can happen if they don't 'grow out of it'. It may be that waiting and seeing how things develop is the right strategy, but not if you arrive at that decision as a result of not wanting the aggravation that might come with intervening.

Pending adulthood demands a great deal of teenagers but, too often, the things we value as parents – their ongoing happiness, their good behaviour, their good manners, even their successes – can count for nothing once they begin to experience the full force of adult life. Josh's hissy fit over being dropped from the school football team is a minor footnote in his history but, as a preparation for adulthood, it was a massive flashing beacon – one which so many of us choose to ignore.

When our children reach adolescence we need to take a deep breath and recalibrate what we are doing. For many parents, adolescence is a series of irritating and exhausting micro-wars about nothing in particular. Parents hang on to the old wives' tale that 'they will grow out of it' eventually and somehow magically acquire the qualities needed to be successful adults along the way. Implicit in this view is that adolescence is a pointless series of hormonal eruptions that need to be endured and nothing else. To my mind it is the most critical period of parenting. Right here in front of us is a fledgling adult arguing that black is white, driving us crazy with his or her demands, but beneath it all wanting to know the answer to one critical question: 'How do I become an adult?'

The more grief and aggravation they cause us, the more anxiety they feel about what lies ahead. We need to make a mental note of where they are in the world and what they lack. If they don't have what it takes to be functioning adults then we have to intervene, sometimes dramatically.

This job is being made harder than ever because, while we are pulling in one direction, the darker more seductive aspects of technology are pulling them in the opposite one. Our best efforts to prepare them for adulthood are being undermined on a daily basis by the addictive and regressive pull of new technologies.

The increase in adolescent mental health problems is evidence of this struggle. Tomorrow's 13-year-olds will almost certainly have spent more time watching a screen than they will have had face-to-face contact with other human beings. What effect this will have on their brain is as yet unclear but you don't have to be a psychologist to surmise that it won't be good. It is critical that we pay close attention to how our adolescents interact with the new technologies, what kind of influence they exert over their lives and how much time they spend with them. For some, that influence will be benign; for others it will be destructive. As a minimum, their use in the home should be ring-fenced in order that the more communal aspects of family life, like meal times and family time, can take place and these children can get some respite from the constant distraction. The enormity of these changes and their potential destructiveness means that we as parents have more actively to engage with our adolescents' daily lives. We need to hold on tighter rather than letting go.

Alongside this we need to worry less about their so-called 'unhappiness', defined in this instance by the desire for perpetual happiness, and concentrate on helping them develop the requisite qualities needed to become competent adults.

It requires us to acquire more subtle skills to avoid being seen as heavy-handed bodyguards. We need to be more vigilant, more attentive, more engaged and more curious. All of this is time-consuming and at times exhausting, but it is nonetheless possible. Our exertions will, ultimately, be rewarded.

At the forefront of our minds is the need to monitor how our work as parents is contributing effectively to our children's capacity to function as adults. Whether they are happy or not during this process is largely irrelevant.

Josh's story is a poignant reminder of what can happen when we sacrifice long-term goals for the sake of short-term peace and happiness. This need not always be the case. Careful parenting during the teenage years can reap amazing benefits.

I am standing on the platform waiting for my train when a tall, elegant, well-dressed young woman taps me on the shoulder and says, 'Hi, Ian.'

I look round but I don't immediately recognise her. She picks up on my surprise.

'It's me, Felicity. You saw me nine years ago, when I was fifteen, remember?'

I do. We sit down on the platform bench and Felicity tells me her story. As she does so, the memories of our work come back to me. She was more or less out of control a decade earlier. She was one of those teenagers who was intent on making the transition to young adulthood in double quick time. Rules were there solely for the purpose of being broken. I remember a time when I thought she would never calm down.

She laughs as she reminds me of the scrapes she got into and the trouble she caused.

'I put my parents through hell. Looking back I feel bad about what I did.'

'Well, from what I see now, that's all in the past. You look as though you are thriving.'

'I am. I eventually went to uni and am now working for an advertising agency and I'm really loving it.'

'So what changed?' I ask. 'What happened to the hell-raiser I knew?'

'Those meetings we had were the start. I think my parents didn't know what to do with me. Looking back, I can see how easy it was to get round them. Everything was a negotiation and I knew I would get my way if I persisted long enough. Don't get me wrong; they loved me to bits but, looking back, I needed them to be stronger with me because I couldn't manage myself. I think they wanted to be my friends rather than my parents. That's why they were so shocked when you suggested laying down ground rules instead of discussing and negotiating everything. They didn't have the stomach for it and didn't believe it would work.'

'As I remember it, we didn't get very far! You ran out of the room and the building when we had that discussion, and that was the last I saw of you.'

'I know, but it was all bravado really, I sort of enjoyed the drama of it. I didn't really have any confidence then. I can see now that all the dramas and trouble were a way of covering up my insecurity and lack of confidence. It all changed when I got arrested for being drunk when I was sixteen. My dad was completely freaked out and so was I. I think that incident frightened him. He and Mum took a completely different stance after that. They started to stand up to me and tried to put into place all the stuff we talked about in those meetings with you. We fought for about a year. It was horrible and I really hated them, but I can see now it was exactly what I needed. It took me forever to realise that losing my freedoms all the time was stupid and pointless, and I started to calm down. Oddly enough, I also started to feel more secure in myself because of it.'

I ask her to tell me more; how she had arrived at the place she inhabits today.

'I didn't do well in my GCSEs, and that hurt a lot, but I pulled it together for A levels and did well. University was fantastic and that's how I'm here, in a job I love and enjoying life.'

Her train arrives and we say goodbye.

The more I reflected on Felicity's story the more remarkable it seemed. I would never have imagined that the out-of-control teenager, the 15-year-old girl, who had run out of my room and the building, could have done so well. I had underestimated her parents and the value of the meetings we did manage to complete. They had shown no evidence of the kind of fortitude and resolve that Felicity described. On the contrary when I met them they were like rabbits in the headlights in the face of their daughter's onslaught. But they made the right choices and turned a potential catastrophe into a success story.

I have listed below what I believe are the top 10 essentials for parenting adolescents. This is by no means a definitive list, but these pointers will give you a framework to think about. If you have these at the forefront of your mind you will find yourself a lot less stressed.

1. **There is no such thing as a turbulence-free adolescence.**

    In fact, it isn't adolescence if there is no conflict or aggravation. The reason is simple: the psychological and emotional work the adolescent has to do is far too demanding and challenging for it to be hassle-free.

They cannot do it without occasional – or in many cases interminable – conflict and argument. If you as a parent of an adolescent don't recognise the relevance of any of the difficulties posed in this book, then there is a problem on your part, not least of which is denial.

2. **However well you think you know your adolescent there will be large parts of their life you will know nothing about.**

It always comes as a shock when parents find out that the child they thought they knew has a whole life going on that they know nothing about. This is a normal part of development and is not a sign of a deceitful adolescent. In order to become independent, adolescents need to have a part of their life that excludes their parents.

3. **Adolescents need parents to be parents; they really do not need their mother or father to be their best mates or friends.**

There is a popular and modern misconception that we need to be 'matey' with our children in order to really understand them and be close to them. This has arisen as a result of a number of factors. Many parents fear being seen as an authority figure and as a consequence don't want to get into conflict with their child. Being an authority figure separates us from our teenagers and puts us in the role of leading them rather than being part of their world. For many parents this is untenable. They feel a need to believe that their children see them as 'cool'. This is utter nonsense; most adolescents think supposedly cool parents are at best an embarrassment and at worst complete idiots. And they have a point.

4. **Heaven, as seen from an adolescent perspective, is complete independence without responsibility.** Your job is to help them understand that with independence comes responsibility. Do not expect them to come on board with the project instantaneously. The job cannot be done overnight; it takes years. Be patient and don't work yourself up into too much of a lather when they fail to marry the two in one easy talking to.

5. **Your job is not to parent in a way that avoids disappointment, upset or conflict but instead to help your adolescent manage these painful feelings.** Stuck record alert: your job as a parent is to prepare your teen for adulthood, not to make them 'happy'. Of course it is painful for any parent to see their child distressed and it is only natural to want to protect them. However, it is worth pausing for a moment in any given situation to try to assess what exactly it is that they are upset or disappointed about. If they haven't done their homework and they are going to get a detention then, no, there is no need to write a letter trying to deflect their teachers from doling out a punishment. It sends completely the wrong message. Likewise, if they auditioned for the school play and didn't make it, they must deal with this as gracefully as possible. Although I know there are plenty of parents who kick up a huge fuss for them on this score, it is doing their children no

favours whatsoever. Life isn't fair. This is a crucial early lesson and learning to manage those feelings of disappointment and upset appropriately is an essential skill for when they grow older. It's perhaps a touch crude but I like the quote attributed to the boxer Mike Tyson: 'Everybody has a plan until they get punched in the mouth.'

6. **Although you will feel helpless from time to time, remember you have one major advantage over your adolescent: you can see the big picture and they manifestly can't.**

   All – indeed the only thing – that is important to them is the here and now. Your overview translates into a useful strategic position: it is fine if you lose a few skirmishes – and, believe me, you will – but if you don't make their youthful mistake of getting too bogged down in the moment, your longer-term outcome can prevail. And if you have been clever about it and avoided too much coercion, the chances are they will lead a more fulfilled life and thank you for it in the end, even if, right now, the 'end' feels as if it is never going to come.

7. **Adolescents have their own internal logic, which isn't logical at all, being as it is largely determined by what they want to have or do right now.**

   So you cannot expect your carefully formulated analyses and reasonable overtures to be met with anything other than disinterest and disdain. Remember, most parent–adolescent dialogues are battles of wills disguised as civilised discussions.

8. **It is not a curtailment of an adolescent's freedom or an infringement of their human rights to have to do what they are told.**

I frequently hear from parents that they like to reason with their adolescent, they like to explain exactly why they have to do something. This inevitably leads to negotiation and debate. As a parenting style this has very little to commend it. It assumes a parity of status, which in reality doesn't exist. It is also used to avoid conflict. It is a style which only works if the teenager agrees with the parental logic. If they don't – and they rarely do – then the parent eventually reverts to screaming and shouting. Believe me, the wiring of the adolescent brain would seem to preclude all presence of logic. Logic goes out of the window and if you insist on using negotiation as a way of managing your child's behaviour it will almost certainly not succeed. In fact, you will feel as if you're forever just 'negotiating' and permanently failing to convey all reason.

9. **You don't have to persecute yourself if you don't get everything right; good enough will do.**

How much we want to get it 'right' depends on many things, particularly our expectations of ourselves – although you might be surprised at how much unconscious competition there is between parents, even among those who claim a complete absence of conscious competition. I well remember feeling intimidated and insecure about my parenting skills as I listened to parents eulogise about their children's startling skills, their model behaviour and astounding intellect. What were these higher beings doing that I wasn't? The more expectations we have of ourselves as parents, the more stress we experience. At its worst, this can be debilitating and create a feeling of inadequacy, a feeling that nothing we do as parents is up to scratch. There is a very real danger that this can communicate itself to your adolescent. He or she feels in turn that nothing they do is good enough and in the long run this is bound to have a harmful effect on their self-esteem. A good enough job is enough for adolescents. Don't worry about mistakes – we all make them by the bucket load.

10. **However grown-up they try to convince you they are, however arrogant and confident they appear, remember it is only skin-deep; mostly it is an act.** Most of the time your adolescent feels anxious, frightened and lost. Don't harp on about their vulnerability and failings; they are only too aware of them. Try instead to understand that their bravado is mostly posturing.

Parenting adolescents can be exhausting, infuriating and time-consuming but it is also hugely entertaining. They can be idealistic and passionate in their beliefs, often absurdly so; their thinking has a sort of fundamentalism to it as in the oft-repeated phrase: 'Oh my God, Mum, I can't believe you just said that.' Their impassioned grand-standing in the face of needing to grow up needs to be understood as preposterous rather than intimidating. They are the epitome of the drama queen. Confrontations will blow over as quickly as they detonate.

If you focus your efforts on their relationships, their work ethic and their emotional resilience and let the rest go you will do a lot more good, have a lot more fun and so will they. However many mistakes you make, however many arguments you have at the end of the process, they will still love you and you them.

Index